How to Open & Operate a
Financially Successful
Landscaping, Nursery, or
Lawn Service Business:
With Companion CD-ROM

How to Open & Operate a Financially Successful Landscaping,
Nursery, or Lawn Service Business: With Companion CD-ROM

Copyright © 2010 Atlantic Publishing Group, Inc.
1405 SW 6th Avenue • Ocala, Florida 34471 • Phone 800-814-1132 • Fax 352-622-1875
Web site: www.atlantic-pub.com • E-mail: sales@atlantic-pub.com
SAN Number: 268-1250

Library of Congress Cataloging-in-Publication Data

How to open & operate a financially successful landscaping, nursery, or lawn service
business : with companion CD-ROM.
    p. cm.
Includes bibliographical references and index.
ISBN-13: 978-1-60138-228-3 (alk. paper)
ISBN-10: 1-60138-228-6 (alk. paper)
1. Landscaping industry--Management. 2. Landscape nurseries--Management. 3. Lawn care
industry--Management. 4. Small business--Management. I. Title: How to open and operate a
financially successful landscaping, nursery, or lawn service business.
 SB472.5.M68 2009
 712.068--dc22
                        2008030019

Printed in the United States

PROJECT MANAGER: Marilee Griffin • mgriffin@atlantic-pub.com
INTERIOR DESIGN: James Ryan Hamilton • www.jamesryanhamilton.com
COVER DESIGN: Meg Buchner • meg@megbuchner.com
JACKET DESIGN: Jackie Miller • sullmill@charter.net
ASSISTANT EDITOR: Angela Pham • apham@atlantic-pub.com

Printed on Recycled Paper

We recently lost our beloved pet "Bear," who was not only our best and dearest friend but also the "Vice President of Sunshine" here at Atlantic Publishing. He did not receive a salary but worked tirelessly 24 hours a day to please his parents. Bear was a rescue dog that turned around and showered myself, my wife, Sherri, his grandparents  Jean, Bob, and Nancy, and every person and animal he met (maybe not rabbits) with friendship and love. He made a lot of people smile every day.

We wanted you to know that a portion of the profits of this book will be donated to The Humane Society of the United States. *–Douglas & Sherri Brown*

The human-animal bond is as old as human history. We cherish our animal companions for their unconditional affection and acceptance. We feel a thrill when we glimpse wild creatures in their natural habitat or in our own backyard.

Unfortunately, the human-animal bond has at times been weakened. Humans have exploited some animal species to the point of extinction.

The Humane Society of the United States makes a difference in the lives of animals here at home and worldwide. The HSUS is dedicated to creating a world where our relationship with animals is guided by compassion. We seek a truly humane society in which animals are respected for their intrinsic value, and where the human-animal bond is strong.

Want to help animals? We have plenty of suggestions. Adopt a pet from a local shelter, join The Humane Society and be a part of our work to help companion animals and wildlife. You will be funding our educational, legislative, investigative and outreach projects in the U.S. and across the globe.

Or perhaps you'd like to make a memorial donation in honor of a pet, friend or relative? You can through our Kindred Spirits program. And if you'd like to contribute in a more structured way, our Planned Giving Office has suggestions about estate planning, annuities, and even gifts of stock that avoid capital gains taxes.

Maybe you have land that you would like to preserve as a lasting habitat for wildlife. Our Wildlife Land Trust can help you. Perhaps the land you want to share is a backyard— that's enough. Our Urban Wildlife Sanctuary Program will show you how to create a habitat for your wild neighbors.

So you see, it's easy to help animals. And The HSUS is here to help.

THE HUMANE SOCIETY
OF THE UNITED STATES.

2100 L Street NW • Washington, DC 20037 • 202-452-1100
www.hsus.org

Trademark Disclaimer

Contents

SECTION FOUR: In The Office 161

Chapter 9: Locating Your Office 163

Chapter 10: Buying Office Equipment and Supplies 167

SECTION FIVE: In The Field 193

Chapter 11: Buying Professional Equipment and Supplies 195

Chapter 12: Hiring Outdoor Workers 219

Introduction

This book does not sell dreams — rather, it shows you, step by step, how to make your personal dream of working for yourself in the outdoors come true. Enterprising owners of outdoor service businesses can make as much as $60 to $80 per hour or more, for up to ten months of the year in the northern climates of the United States — or for all 12 months if you are willing to plow snow. That is decent money.

As a business owner, you are in control of your destiny. However, ownership does not make the work easier — it may even seem harder sometimes. But if you like the feeling responsibility, you will never be afraid of layoffs again because, as the boss, you are in charge. When you come up with a new idea you can experiment, watch what happens, and learn from the results. You do not have to get permission.

The business can grow with you, at your own pace. Age is not a drawback — from high school students to grandparents, anyone who can push a lawnmower (or hire someone else to push one) can enter the outdoor service business. The cost of entry is remarkably low. Some lawn care specialists started businesses with little more than a single lawnmower.

Of course, easy, low-cost entry means lots of competition. You will have to hone your competitive skills. According to US Census Bureau statistics, in 2006 over 89,000 landscaping firms operated in the US with nearly 567,000 paid employees. Of this group, 65,435 of these firms had fewer than four employees; yet combined, they generated over $3 billion in annual payroll. But there is a growing demand for outdoor services as the nation becomes more environmentally conscious and recognizes that lawns, flowers, and trees are more than beautiful — they cleanse the very air we breathe. As our population ages, more lawn care work is hired out. A National Gardening Association survey reported that between 2001 and 2006, US households increased their expenditure on lawn and landscape services from $24.5 billion to $44.7 billion. That is nearly double!

If you have courage and determination, you will soon be a part of this trend. You are about to become part of the green culture by contributing your hard work, love of nature, personal drive, and need for independence toward a business achievement of your very own.

Although no book can do the grunt work for you, if you truly care about creating and building a landscape, lawn care, or nursery business, by the time you are finished reading this book, you will have a plan of action ready and understand most of the challenges ahead. You will also know where to look for additional answers. The nine sections that follow are organized for a person new to the business. Through step-by-step instructions, they will help you establish a plan and solid foundation for your company. Once you gain your footing by doing things "by the book," you can and should open the door to innovation by experimenting with your own methods and ideas. That is what will help you establish your distinctive business "personality," which has the potential to attract customers that fit you best.

It will not be long before you are equipped to launch and run an outdoor service business, organized in a way that makes sense to you. By applying consistent, methodical effort, you will quickly strip away the distracting clutter that interferes with sound business development and management.

The following list offers a sneak peek into the instructions offered inside these pages:

How to run a successful business: one that makes money and pleases your customers, while bringing you satisfaction and a sense of accomplishment along with an income.

How to work efficiently, getting the most value from every hour and dollar you spend.

What is involved in the different types of outdoor service businesses. Find who has the answers to your problems, and learn how to stay informed about the industry on both local and national levels.

The basics of business structure and startup. What you need to get going, and how to keep all the government agencies happy so you can get on with the work you love.

The right equipment, procedures, and practices necessary to launch your business and get it headed toward success.

How to schedule time, write contracts, and plan for expenses. Learn how and where to borrow money.

Secret low-cost or no-cost marketing tips that will inspire customers to sign up with your company.

Procedures that encourage your existing customers to become your personal recruiters for new customers.

The ethical business owner's creed: how the goodwill you receive from giving back to the community and treating people fairly pays off in dollars, as well as respect.

These are just a few highlights; there is much, much more to learn and absorb. But by opening the cover of this book, you are already positioning yourself for a successful, long-lasting career in the great outdoors. You have probably heard that phrase, "time is money." If you can teach yourself one extra business skill in addition to your outdoor specialties, learning how to make time work for you, not against you, is a profitable activity.

Start practicing efficient time management right now by reading this book in the way that is of greatest benefit to you. There is no one right way to approach this. True, this book lays out a step-by-step plan for people brand-new to business operations, but look at the table of contents before you begin, and start in the middle if a topic draws you in. For instance, if you have owned a business before and have a basic understanding of record keeping, move on to topics that are less familiar. If you have previously written business plans, you may be able to skim the business plan section for new ideas, or if you already know which aspect of the outdoor services industry suits you, then it is fine to save Section II for last. Remember that you are not going to be graded by a teacher for your knowledge of this material. Instead, you will be graded when you interact with your first customer, make your first bank deposit, work with your first employee, and file taxes for the first time. This book can be the starting point for your personal growth, so it deserves your serious concentration. The Case Studies that are scattered throughout the book provide real-life advice and show you how others have achieved their dreams. You can too.

CASE STUDY: GREEN GARDENS, MARK MCCUNE

Green Gardens, Inc.
P. O. Box 189 Clarksburg, MD 20871
301-972-9090

Green Gardens is what co-owner Mark McCune describes as a "blue chip garden company." Green
Gardens targets upscale homeowners who want
more than mowed lawns and weed-free flowerbeds. The company has about
100 customers in the affluent neighborhoods of Washington, D.C., Montgomery
County, Maryland, and in Northern Virginia. Services include elegant designs by
landscape architect Tom Hamm, whose work appears in the photographs found
in this book.

Green Gardens was founded in the mid-1960s by two men who decided to strike
out on their own after working at another landscaping company. Both men were
gifted landscapers and one of them was also a talented salesman, said Mc-
Cune. Right from the start, both men knew the market they wanted: upscale,
private residences.

McCune joined the company in the mid-1970s, first as a landscape worker and
later as co-owner. The original owners are long gone, but the focus of the company remains "blue chip." He believes that the key to a landscaping company's
success is having one small area of expertise and being good at it. In Green Gardens' case, their niche is garden design and maintenance. The company does
not apply chemicals; instead, it works with subcontractors to provide chemical
applications. Nor does it operate a nursery to retail plants. "We just plant the
stuff," McCune said.

Green Gardens has developed a network of vendors and subcontractors that
allow the company to focus on its core services, while still offering customers
the products and other elements that are necessary for a beautiful and well-
maintained garden. These suppliers include nurseries that grow and deliver the
plants that Green Gardens uses in its landscape designs. Even with its upscale
customers, Green Gardens deals with the most common question customers
ask: "How can we save money?" Smaller plants, delaying some projects, or
waiting until next year, are some of the answers McCune offers.

Green Gardens does *no* marketing. None. That is the benefit of years of customer
satisfaction. McCune says existing customers and word-of-mouth keep the company busy with maintenance and new design contracts.

SECTION ONE

Choosing the Outdoor Business That Is Right for You

Chapter One

Characteristics of a Successful Business

The following six factors are essential to the long-term success of any business, outdoor or otherwise:

- Passion is the prime ingredient. A successful business is "more than a business" to its owner.

- A solid business foundation is built on a well-considered strategic plan.

- Excellent customer relations are the hallmark of success.

- Quality, reliability, and service are emphasized.

- Procedures, products, pricing, and all the strategic necessities of the business are regularly evaluated and monitored by the owner.

- A flexible business remains successful as it adapts readily to changes in the industry, technology, and market.

Let us examine each one of these critical factors more closely. Take the first factor: passion. Think about what spurred you to purchase this book. Was it merely idle curiosity? Probably not. More likely, you feel driven from the inside out to forge your own path and create an enterprise that serves your needs for secure income and a sense of purpose. That is the meaning of passion.

Successful business owners feel passionately about the products and services they provide. The profits matter, of course, but there is more to a business than profitability. The business has meaning for the owner. It is part of his or her identity. It can be all-consuming, even a preoccupation — and sometimes, this can be too much of a good thing. But the energy and the passion that underlie a successful business are channeled into all the other factors that set it apart from a mediocre business.

Realistically, running an outdoor service business takes a lot of hard, often physical work. Take landscaping: wrestling trees into the ground, maneuvering heavy equipment, and carting heavy bags of mulch are tasks for those who do not mind getting dirty or ending their days physically exhausted. Operating a nursery with the objective of raising flowers, shrubs, trees, or all three can be a worrisome battle with weather, plant diseases, pests, and customer indifference. Lawn care and yard maintenance have their downsides too, like sweat, equipment breakdowns, and stiff competition keeping you awake at night.

But if you find meaning and a sense of purpose in creating a beautiful setting through nurturing flowers and trees, landscaping, or spending time in the fresh air while you manicure yards and commercial properties, then you will have the drive to find the labor invigorating, the repetitive work a form of meditation, and the challenging work a source of personal growth.

The second factor, a solid business foundation, is obvious. But what does this really mean?

A solid business is one that is funded sufficiently and has access to competent professionals for consultation or ongoing work in legal, accounting, tax, and banking arenas. It has sufficient insurance coverage and operates appropriately within the local, state, and national legal requirements. Its office maintains accurate records that are easy to find when needed. If it has employees, they are well trained, perform quality work, and respect customers. The equipment is kept in good-working order. Its customers are pleased with its service, and are glad to recommend this business to family and friends.

A solid business is operated using a strategic plan developed by the owner and management team. It specifies short, mid-range, and long-term goals for the company, and proposes a method or multiple methods to achieve these goals. The strategic plan is not a one-time effort. It is a living document that is modified as new situations develop and demand change.

The third and fourth characteristics are joint-profitability components defined by excellent customer relations and quality, reliability, and service orientation. Most customers today are looking for value. They want friendly people working on their yards and green spaces. They want return guarantees on nursery plants that die shortly after planting. They hate sloppy work, poor clean up, or missed appointments. Today's customers demand top-quality service, and appreciate companies that give a little extra attention to detail.

Factor five in the list of critical factors for a successful business is the owner's ongoing commitment to evaluating, monitoring, and improving business performance. An ability to pinch pennies without sacrificing quality, reliability, and service is something all successful business owners demonstrate. It may be second nature, or it may be acquired through trial and error, but it needs to be present. A wise business owner schedules system-wide evaluations of the business' functions. At minimum, there will be an annual price comparison with local and national competitors in the field. There will be customer surveys to solicit feedback. Cost and condition of all materials, equipment, and employee services will be examined at least once a year.

In large corporations, top executives often stress "management by walking around." In small but successful companies, the owners constantly stay aware of what is going on within their business and its relationship to customers, vendors, repair people, competitors, partners, and relevant government regulators. By connecting with the touchstones of their business from the very beginning, they are able to make appropriate decisions with less strain.

The last factor, flexibility, is a result of a business-owner picking up on changes in the marketplace. Changes in technology, government regulation, and customer preference have been frequent and dramatic over the last few decades. We have seen the end of cheap gasoline, the rise of green power and green consciousness, and the birth and incredible growth of the Internet. This is an era of organic awareness and economy, and big lawns may soon include self-grown vegetable gardens (another possible profit center for enterprising outdoor service companies). Every month seems to bring out new software products for business management, new equipment choices, fertilizers, and pesticides — and the regulation of these products require smart decision-making on the part of business owners. Making necessary corrections to your business model is like a dance, and you do not want to trip. Not every adjustment will be an improvement, but by keeping close tabs on changes, the smart business owner makes rapid corrections to a situation before it does serious damage to his company's profits or community reputation.

Chapter Two

Know Yourself Before You Start a Business

Almost everyone has dreamed of owning his or her own business. Oftentimes, these dreams are the result of dealing with difficult bosses, low pay, long hours, swing shifts, and other frustrations that come from working for someone else. In the safe confines of the imagination, the vision of owning a business is immensely satisfying: you are your own boss, you make your own decisions, and you do not have to answer to anyone else. What could be better?

While there are elements of truth in this dream-world vision of business ownership, it is also true that in reality, business owners have problems too. The problems are different from the frustrations faced by employees, but they are serious and stomach wrenching just the same. You will want to know your personal capacity to deal with the problems of business ownership before you jump out of the workforce and take over the boss's chair.

For example: imagine hiring a person you really like as a human being. This person is very pleasant and, as far as you can tell, tries hard to do a good job. Maybe he or she is a personal friend. But what if that individual is not performing a job assignment correctly, angers an important customer, or pads expenses or hours? How will you handle it? Will you simply fire that person on the spot, or will you have a talk with him or her? If you decide to have a talk, do you know what you will say? If you do not know what to say, where will you go to find a suitable approach? Will this conflict mark the end of a long, rewarding friendship? Even if you know this individual needs to be let go, do you have the stomach to do it? That is one type of "boss problem" you may find yourself facing. Here is another:

Imagine you get a lucky break. You have been doing most of the work yourself, but your marketing efforts pay off big time and suddenly you have too much work. You need to hire someone, fast. Where will you find this person? He or she needs to be reliable (this person must show up for the job on time or your customers will be angry), and trustworthy (this person will be in charge of expensive equipment, so what if he or she takes off with it?) Your new hire must also be respectful of the customer, be quality conscious, and follow instructions — you do not want to damage your reputation by employing the wrong person. Will you place a classified ad and, if so, how will you judge the people who apply for the job? Will you call the local temporary labor service pool for a part-time employee to test out? Will you ask friends and family to recommend someone? If you hire a referral from friends or family, how will you treat that referral so as not to damage or destroy an existing relationship if the individual does not satisfy your work requirements?

Finally, here is a third dilemma: You have lots of work, things are going well, but as always, you are short on cash. One morning, just as you are getting ready to start the day's work, your primary truck — the one you purchased used to save money when you started the business — breaks down again for the umpteenth time. What will you do? Will you replace it, or will you try to fix the broken-down truck yet again? Can you afford a new truck, or will you buy used again? If so, where will you get the money to pay for it? Do you have enough set aside to pay cash? In the meantime, what do you do about the customers you have scheduled for today's work? Will you call and tell them you are in a bind and will come as soon as possible, or will you not call and hope they do not remember you were supposed to be there? Will you lease a truck for a few days (or a few months) to keep the workflow on schedule? If so, where does the lease money come from and who exactly will give you the best deal for that short-term lease?

This is just a brief glimpse at the problems of business ownership. Day after day, problems large and small crop up, and as the boss, you are the person who must decide what to do. You may ask professionals for advice. You may consult with your spouse, your accountant, your banker, or your best friend — but as the owner and operator of this business, you are ultimately in charge. It is your decision, period. So if you are the type of person who would really rather let your employee decide what to do than take charge of the project yourself, then you could be a superb manager but not really have the personality to own a business.

Franchise or From the Ground Up?

Do you hate to have other people tell you what to do? Do you have ideas for how your business would be "different," or are you happier if someone gives you a blueprint to follow? Your answers to these questions will help you decide if you would rather start your own operation, or open a franchise instead.

Are you a "ground-up initiator," or would you rather walk into a company that already has a track record and some customers — a place where you could either go with what is established, or apply changes more slowly? Everyone has different preferences, and you need to consider your preferences carefully before deciding whether to start a company from scratch or buy into a small, established operation instead.

What is your energy level? Have you heard the joke about the self-employed? "Yeah, I make my own schedule. I get to decide which 80 hours of the week I work." Are you a born manager or are you more "hands-on?" Do you like numbers, especially if they involve money? Do you like to talk to people, or are you a silent, get-it-done kind of person? Can you delegate? Do you want to do everything yourself? What do you like to do, and what do you hate doing? If you have thought all this through, skip the following checklist. But if you have not really considered some of these factors, do it now. *You* are the core of your potential new business, and you will need to know your preferences so all the gaps are filled as you make future decisions.

Franchise

If you choose the franchise option, you will be buying an existing business model and getting some training and support, at least for your first months. Of course, there will likely be monthly franchise fees, national advertising fees, and other expenses that you would not incur with a startup business of your own. You will also be subject to the rules, standards, and protocols of the franchiser, who will dictate to some degree what you can and cannot do with "your" business. (Some truly independent business owners may find it unacceptable to have a long-distance boss overseeing their work.)

For example, U.S. Lawns, based in Orlando, Fla., claims more than 200 franchises nationwide. On its Web site, the company says it is one of the nation's "fastest-growing landscape maintenance franchise companies and the landscape maintenance industry's only registered franchise organization." The key word here is "maintenance." The company's Web site lists such services as turf maintenance, fertilization, insect and disease control, and small tree pruning. U.S. Lawns has carved out its niche and does not offer the large-scale landscape design and construction option other companies offer, but it has a focus and a market, which it will share it with you if you buy a franchise. The cost is between $50,000 and $100,000, plus whatever fees and expenses are required through your franchise agreement.

Lawn Doctor is another franchise opportunity for landscapers. Lawn Doctor specializes in lawn, tree, and shrub care and it manufactures its own equipment, which franchisers are expected to use. Some franchise opportunities are quite specialized. Southwest Greens of Scottsdale, Ariz. offers golf green and synthetic turf installation and design.

If you think franchising is the way to go, you will want to expend serious effort researching various franchises. Visit a franchise outlet — preferably some distance from your location — and talk candidly with the operator. Also, use the Internet to identify Web sites or blogs that discuss particular franchises. Get input from people who are enjoying the franchise, and those who have problems with it — the so-called "disgruntled buyers." You do not want to go into a franchise purchase without a clear idea of the pros and cons.

Purchasing an existing business

As with a franchise, if you buy an existing business, you are buying a current business model. It may or may not be a good deal, depending on the person who is selling the business and how it has been run. When you buy an existing landscaping business, you are acquiring a customer list, some equipment, a reputation, and possibly an ongoing contract or two. In theory, you will be buying something that is already producing income. If this is true, it will eliminate the intense pressure to get money flowing in right away. Of course, you will need to keep your business going and continue to build it up. The first consideration in buying an existing business is price. How much can you spend? What are you getting for the money?

Here are prices of landscaping businesses that were for sale on **BizBuySell.com** in the fall of 2007:

- A Florida retail garden and landscape business was offered for $4,000,000 with a cash flow greater than $800,000. Cash flow is a way of describing the profit available to the owner. If you are interested in buying an existing business, have a professional examine the numbers. Cash flow can be a slippery issue and owners' claims must be verified.

- Also in Florida, a lawn maintenance business was listed for $175,000 and claimed over $80,000 in cash flow. The price included two dump trucks, a trailer, a handful of commercial accounts, and a few dozen residential customers. The owner said he was turning business away. You should be skeptical about business owner statements. It is unlikely that an owner is going to admit that his business is going under and he is selling because he cannot take the downward spiral any longer.

- In New Jersey, a "successful landscaping business" was advertised for $80,000. It came with trucks, equipment, and 22 customers. The owner claimed a cash flow of $60,000. That comes out to just under $2,800 per customer per year.

If you are considering buying a business, look carefully at the business' numbers for the last two or three years. Pay close attention to tax returns and the expense/income reporting. Do not be shy about asking questions such as, "Is this business making any money?" Regardless of the answers you receive, be sure a competent accountant inspects the books. This is especially necessary if it sounds too good to be true.

Remember that when you buy an existing business, part of the purchase price is the goodwill of the person selling it. There are no real guarantees that he or she will not take the customer list with them, along with your check. You may want to draft a "no-compete" clause in the sale contract to ensure the old owner does not raid your business after you take over. It is up to you whether you want the old owner to assist you during the break-in period.

If you can get along with each other, this could be a substantial help during the initial phase of your new occupation. But if there is reluctance or ambivalence coming from either side, you may be better off to just dive in on your own.

Starting from scratch

If you plan to start your business from scratch you are on your own, however, your costs are lower and you will not have to follow the plans and policies of a franchise, or deal with the reputation of a previous business owner. You will be in complete control, and will have the prospect of success or of failure on your shoulders. It will be up to you to find customers, market your services, research your vendors and potential partners, hire any employees, and set up your office. This is a huge challenge, but if you have a vision in mind, you may be eager to take it on. Remember – planning is key.

CASE STUDY: SAVATREE, MIKE NEWMAN

SavATree 19 offices from Virginia to Massachusetts
www.savatree.com

SavATree is a tree and lawn care company specializing in what Massachusetts-area manager Mike Newman calls "full plant health care." The company does far more than trim dead limbs from trees. SavATree applies fertilizers and pesticides to feed trees, shrubs and lawns, and eliminate the pests that can destroy them.

SavATree does not plant trees or shrubs, just cares for them. This means long-term contracts with homeowners, golf courses, schools, parks, and other areas where specialized care is needed.

The company has been in business for 25 years and has around 450 employees on the payroll at the height of the season, which begins in spring. SavATree offers intense training, with an emphasis on safety — company policy requires

CASE STUDY: SAVATREE, MIKE NEWMAN

a full investigation into all mishaps, such as a branch falling onto a patio and cracking the stone or a limb accidentally breaking a window.

The company carries all required insurance coverage and is a member of state, national, and international arborist associations.

SavATree's marketing includes targeting mailings and building relationships with potential commercial accounts. Newman says SavATree was built on long-term relationships that require excellent customer service.

The company's pricing is "on the higher end of the scale," according to Newman, but provides "more for the dollar," meaning the assurance that customers are dealing with a fully licensed and insured professional plant care company. Prices vary by season, with the slow winter period offering lower rates to bring in enough business to keep crews busy. Peak season services can be pricier, but customers can enjoy discounts by agreeing to long-term contracts that bundle services such as trimming, fertilizing, and pesticides.

As with other commercial landscape and plant companies, SavATree must deal with unlicensed and untrained competitors who offer low prices, but whose knowledge and safety policies are often severely lacking. One way to offset this challenge is to inform customers that unlicensed and often unscrupulous operators can produce more problems than they solve.

Personality Quiz

I am happiest when I am completely in charge of a project and using my own ideas.

(Yes___ Sometimes___ No___)

I prefer to have a group of people brainstorm alternatives and then come to a group consensus to set priorities and make decisions.

(Yes___ Sometimes___ No___)

I like to have someone else with more experience set my targets and goals, so I can meet or exceed them.

(Yes___ Sometimes___ No___)

I am excited about starting from scratch.

(Yes___ Sometimes___ No___)

I enjoy building teams as long as I am the leader.

(Yes___ Sometimes___ No___)

I feel uptight if someone asks me a question and I do not immediately know the answer.

(Yes___ Sometimes___ No___)

I enjoy pleasing the people I work for.

(Yes___ Sometimes___ No___)

I want to help my employees feel successful and I know how to encourage others.

(Yes___ Sometimes___ No___)

My primary goal is to make a lot of money fast, and have lots of leisure time.

(Yes___ Sometimes___ No___)

I like the idea of coming to work later in the morning and seeing my employees already working.

(Yes___ Sometimes___ No___)

I know I do not know how to do everything, but I am willing to ask for advice and even pay for it.

(Yes___ Sometimes___ No___)

I would rather learn on the job by trial and error than pay for help.

(Yes___ Sometimes___ No___)

I would rather sit in my office making phone calls and setting appointments than working outside, getting sweaty.

(Yes___ Sometimes___ No___)

I do not care if I have to follow someone else's rules if I benefit from their expertise and make more money faster.

(Yes___ Sometimes___ No___)

I work outdoors, and I play outdoors. It is my favorite place to be.

(Yes___ Sometimes___ No___)

I hate being cooped up in an office.

(Yes___ Sometimes___ No___)

I have excellent mechanical skills.

(Yes___ Sometimes___ No___)

I know I am good at what I do, but I know my limits.

(Yes___ Sometimes___ No___)

I am orderly by nature. I live by the motto: "a place for everything and everything in its place."

(Yes___ Sometimes___ No___)

Even if my work area seems messy, it is organized to suit my needs.

(Yes___ Sometimes___ No___)

I like the challenge of getting along with difficult people.

(Yes___ Sometimes___ No___)

One of my goals is to inspire others to succeed. I want to be a role model in my community.

(Yes___ Sometimes___ No___)

I would like a job where I can get my hands dirty.

(Yes___ Sometimes___ No___)

I prefer the wilderness to a manicured golf course.

(Yes___ Sometimes___ No___)

I keep my checkbook balanced and promptly reconcile bank statements.

(Yes___ Sometimes___ No___)

I pay my taxes on time.

(Yes___ Sometimes___ No___)

I know the local regulations for the business I want to open.

(Yes___ Sometimes___ No___)

I feel comfortable negotiating prices with customers and vendors.

(Yes___ Sometimes___ No___)

I like to associate with people from different backgrounds.

(Yes___ Sometimes___ No___)

I will tell an employee the end result I want, and let him figure out how to achieve it.

(Yes___ Sometimes___ No___)

I am rarely satisfied, and I always strive for improvement.

(Yes___ Sometimes___ No___)

I have always enjoyed working with numbers.

(Yes___ Sometimes___ No___)

I am willing to change any business practice or product at a moment's notice if I hear of something that might work better.

(Yes___ Sometimes___ No___)

I hate having someone else tell me what to do or how to do it.

(Yes___ Sometimes___ No___)

I am done with formal education forever.

(Yes___ No___ Maybe___)

I will ask customers for feedback regularly. If I do not hear complaints, I will not change anything in the business.

(Yes___ Sometimes___ No___)

I like to shop for bargains.

(Yes___ Sometimes___ No___)

I do not take chances; I plan for all possibilities.

(Yes___ Sometimes___ No___)

I can be OK without a regular paycheck for a while.

(Yes___ Sometimes___ No___)

I am eager to open this business. It is like a parachute jump—a leap into the unknown.

(Yes___ Sometimes___ No___)

I have enough of my own money and resources to start this business immediately.

(Yes___ Sometimes___ No___)

I know where to get more money if I need it.

(Yes___ Sometimes___ No___)

I am living from paycheck to paycheck now. I am tired of it.

(Yes___ Sometimes___ No___)

I want customers ready and waiting the day I open my doors.

(Yes___ Sometimes___ No___)

I have many ideas about marketing my business and I know how to get it done.

(Yes___ Sometimes___ No___)

I already have a company name picked out.

(Yes___ No___)

I already know what kind of customers I want to serve.

(Yes___ No___)

I dream about this business at night.

(Yes___ Sometimes___ No___)

I have a picture in my head of me running my own business.

(Yes___ Sometimes___ No___)

My family and friends are supportive of my business ideas.

(Yes___ Sometimes___ No___)

Scoring:

Business ownership may be appropriate for you if you answered "yes" on questions 1, 4, 5, 8, 12, 33, 34, 39, 41, 42, 48, 49, and 50. This response shows that you have an independent spirit and are willing to take full responsibility for the job you are undertaking. A "yes" response on question 2 suggests that you might want to form a partnership, or at least consider bringing employees, family, or other advisors to help you make business decisions.

A person well suited to franchise ownership might answer "yes" to questions 3, 14, and 50. Someone who answers "yes" to 41, 42, and 44 may find purchasing an existing business more appropriate than starting from scratch. Delegating skills are highlighted by "yes" answers to questions 18 and 30.

A good attitude that will be helpful in business is demonstrated by "yes" answers to questions 11, 21, 22, 38, and 40. Skills and affinities useful to business operation are shown in "yes" answers to 15, 16,17, 19, 20, 23, 25, 26, 27, 28, 29, 31, 32, 37, 45, 46, and 47.

Finally, those who answer "yes" to questions 9, 10, 13, 24, 35, 36, and 43 may find the reality of business ownership difficult. This does *not* mean you cannot run a successful business, just as a "no" to certain questions in the skills and affinities group does not mean you cannot succeed. But, it *does* mean that you may need to select partners, advisors, or get some specific training yourself to make the path of your business growth possible and realistic. It is always helpful to consider delegating work that is in an area where your skills are not supreme. Also, remember that showing your employees that you are dedicated to doing the job will inspire them to make their best effort, too.

SECTION TWO
Outdoor Opportunities

Chapter Three

The Nitty Gritty Work of Landscaping

The landscaping business sector includes everything from one man with a lawnmower and leaf blower to the high-end companies that offer landscape architectural services and patio, pond, and waterfall construction. Their common denominator is outdoor work, with plants and greenery. To launch a successful outdoor service business, you must first define what it is you want to be doing, and how you will proceed towards that goal. If you see yourself as a landscaping professional, you must know what that work entails.

Landscaping businesses may be found in the phone book or on the Web, categorized under many different names. Listings are offered for landscape designers, landscape architects, landscape contractors, and landscape gardeners, among others. The scope of work provided by each of these different types of companies may vary according to the owner's preference. Most frequently though, a landscaping professional looks at the yard or garden, plans it out, obtains customer approval, and then performs or subcontracts the various steps required to fulfill the agreed-upon design.

The job of a typical landscape designer or architect is to consult with the property owner, listen carefully to his or her vision for the space involved, and finally draw up plans that incorporate the customer's vision, tastes, and needs within the budget. The designer or architect may be responsible for outlining walkways and locating and specifying statuary, gazebos, trellises or other landscape features, defining flower gardens and specifying particular plants, shrubs, or trees. The landscape professional may also determine sources of water, locations for lighting, electrical outlets, and gas connections for grills.

Even if your long-term goal is to focus on landscape design as a whole, the "big picture" of the business, you may find yourself beginning with smaller clients who have a single small project. You will need to decide if you want to handle the construction details that may be needed — building walls, laying flagstone walks, erecting fences, or building decks. You may also want to consider how to handle the situation if a customer wants to do part of the work themselves.

A "landscape contractor" is usually prepared to do the grading, heavy earth moving, lifting, and rearranging that may be desired to enhance the landscape terrain. This means the ownership or rental of compact excavators, bulldozers, dump trucks, and other earth-moving necessities, as well as skilled operators.

The opportunities for landscape professionals are growing. National Gardening Association's 2006 Lawn and Landscaping Survey found that one-third of all U.S. households hired a lawn and landscape professional. Homeowners spend nearly 45 billion dollars a year to create the beautiful yards and gardens that enhance their property and increase its value.

After interviewing the property owner, a professional landscaper returns to the office to research costs for materials, plants, labor, installation, and other factors that go into the project. After projecting these costs, marking up items acquired from vendors and adding a sum for administration, the quote will be ready for your customer. You will also want to present the customer with a timetable along with the quote. In the pricing section in Chapter 8 you will learn more about how to set a rate, but at this point it is just good to remind you that the cheapest estimate may not always be the best. Underestimating costs is the sign of a careless, inexperienced landscaper who will have a hard time growing a successful business. The more details you can specify, the more accurate the quote will be.

The owner of a landscape gardening business is responsible for creating beautiful gardens and a healing atmosphere that uplifts customer's spirits. By creating a calming influence, this profession provides a refuge from life's stresses.

Landscape architects are often specially trained and licensed individuals who coordinate planning and design on many scales. They may or may not provide their own service for the planting of flowerbeds, ornamental shrubs, and trees. Sometimes they are partners with professional landscape gardeners or nurseries that handle the actual installation of the selected plants.

Every state has its own requirements for landscape contractors. On your state's official Web site, you will find specific information about licensing and other requirements to become a professional landscaper as you define the role.

You may have decided to go into business for yourself because you were tired of following the rules set out by an employer, but even business owners have to play by the rules established by government entities. There are federal guidelines about paying taxes for your business, yourself, and your employees. The federal government also insists you pay minimum wages, deposit the employer portion of social security for each employee, and do not discriminate in hiring. The EPA regulates storage, application, and disposal of fertilizers, pesticides, and other chemical treatments for lawns, and OSHA administers safety practices.

At the state and local level, business rules vary according to jurisdiction. Every state and municipality has a department of business development that will gladly instruct you about the rules you need to follow. There may be zoning considerations, city tax filings, personal property taxes, or vendor's licenses that are necessary to operate your business within the laws of your community. It is a good idea to set aside a day or two of research and planning several weeks before you plan to offer your services to the public. Make the necessary phone calls or online registrations needed to acquire the facts about business rules you must follow. Keep notes and copies of the papers you filed in labeled folders so you can find them in the future.

Doing a Good Job Is Not Enough

Even if you have considerable experience with planting and landscape design and know that this work is your "calling," it may not be enough to make your business successful. Excellent customer relations, sound marketing techniques, and a profit-oriented approach are essentials that the "garden artist" side of you may not have developed yet. Planning your business and setting goals are tasks that may seem less important at first than creating a breathtakingly beautiful landscape. But going with the flow will not lead you to success. You are smart to set goals. These goals need to include the services and products you will provide, a step-by-step plan to ready the business for the goals you have set, and a plan for obtaining any additional training and licensing you may require.

Remember, too, that it costs less to keep an existing client than for you to develop a positive relationship with a new customer. Everything you do to build and strengthen your first homeowner or commercial account can lead to additional work and future referrals. The best advertising for any business is word of mouth. Turning your clients into friends is a positive way to make your workday more pleasant, and improve your chances for business success at the same time.

Outdoor Maintenance

You are reading this book because you want to take mowing and yard care seriously. The simplest startup in the outdoor services business is mowing lawns. This is an easy, entry-level business suitable at its most primitive level for practically anyone with a lawn mower, from teens to grandparents. But if you are considering lawn care and maintenance as a serious part-time or full-time venture, you will want to think it through as carefully as if you were going to open a complicated landscaping or nursery business.

It is relatively easy to build a profitable small lawn mowing business. Grass never stops growing, and homeowners frequently get tired of going out and pushing a mower themselves. If you want to make this work as economical for you as possible, target a specific neighborhood that has small size lawns — one-third acre or less. These are quick to mow, easy to price competitively, and if you build some skill at sales, you can acquire several customers close to each other to make your mowing more efficient. We will discuss pricing more completely in Chapter 8, but for now consider this rule of thumb: a quarter-acre of lawn should take fewer than 60 minutes to mow. Customers will often accept the idea of a flat fee for small yards rather than an hourly rate. Your rate of return may be much more substantial if you can do five-to-seven yards per day (or more) charging per job, rather than just one or two billed per hour. So look for those small lawns, as well as areas around gas stations and other commercial properties.

A serious yard maintenance business will involve more than just pushing the mower. There will be raking and bagging the yard clippings, edging sidewalks and around flower beds, pulling or whacking weeds along fences — and for some customers, cleaning up flower beds, clipping hedges, and trimming shrubs. You may also be asked to collect and dispose of the twigs and branches left after a storm, clean up pet areas, and other tasks that are essential to making your customer's yard look pleasant and pristine.

You have to identify and factor into your expenses all the materials you will be using to perform each job, such as plastic bags, equipment like yard tools and mower(s), and supplies such as oil and gasoline. Add them all together and then divide by the number of contracts to figure an average of your expenses versus your income. It is even more helpful for your business profitability if you chart the expenditures on a per-yard basis to determine which aspects of yard work are the most profitable for you. Do you make more per hour if you do pet clean up, for example (charging extra, of course)? Or is that just too much labor to pay off?

You may be able to garner an extra fee for unpleasant or time-consuming jobs, such as mucking-out a garden pool, or performing minor fence repairs. If your customers see you as a service person with multiple skills, you will have to decide if the payoff is worth it. Some yard maintenance businesses are glad to accept the extra responsibilities. Others prefer to focus on yard cutting, period. At the outset, you may want to explore this on a case-by-case basis. It is helpful to have friends or relatives in the neighborhood(s) you select who would like you to cut their yards. If you satisfy your first customers, you begin to build the word-of-mouth referrals that will fill your schedule.

Yard maintenance also includes the autumn leaf-raking season in northern climates. Other potential homeowner requests include mulching and digging up plants that are not winter-hardy for cold-weather storage to be replanted in spring. If you live in locations with a winter season, you may be able to make a year-round income from your spring and summer customers by offering snowplowing, shoveling, or de-icing services for sidewalks and driveways. Again, you will need to consider equipment and materials cost when deciding what to charge.

CASE STUDY: UNLIMBITED TREE SERVICE INC., CHUCK PRESLIPSKY

UnLIMBited Tree Service Inc.
8448 Alvin Road
Pasadena, MD 21122
410-360-1618
http://unlimbitedtreeservice.com

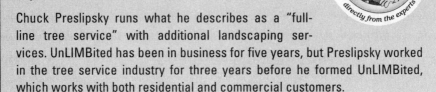

Chuck Preslipsky runs what he describes as a "full-line tree service" with additional landscaping services. UnLIMBited has been in business for five years, but Preslipsky worked in the tree service industry for three years before he formed UnLIMBited, which works with both residential and commercial customers.

Preslipsky is fully licensed and has four full-time and two part-time employees. His services include: removal of limbs or entire trees, installing tree support systems and lightening protection, deep root feeding, and even stump grinding. Most of his employees have some training in tree maintenance when he hires them, but he provides continued training with a heavy emphasis on safety.

Landscaping services were added to the tree services because, as he puts it, "When you're looking at removal of a 40-thousand pound tree, it will have an impact on the landscape." Preslipsky's company offers long-term landscape maintenance that includes spring cleanup and mulching, a specified number of annuals and perennials, and a fall cleanup — all for a set fee.

UnLIMBited does not offer leaf removal in the fall because Preslipsky has not been able to find a recycling center that will accept leaves, although the recycling center he uses will accept tree debris. His company does not provide lawn-mowing services either because Preslipsky realized he would have to set up a separate division of business to make it work for him. He found that he would need 40-to-50 lawn mowing accounts to make a profit, so UnLIMBited Tree Service is currently servicing existing customers who contract with other companies to mow their lawns; Preslipsky concentrates on their trees and flowers.

UnLIMBited's marketing is through the Internet, the telephone book, and of course, referrals.

Chapter Four

The Nursery Business

Green is "In"

Plant production is the basis of the nursery business. Committing oneself full-time to growing plants for a living without a set of established customers requires either a tremendous leap of faith or a well-stocked bank account. However, do not underestimate the value that homeowners place on the colorful plants and greenery in their yards and gardens. The US Agricultural Census for 2007 notes sales surpassing $20 billion for US-grown nursery products, excluding seeds, vegetables, and sod.

A few of the pitfalls of running a garden center or nursery include: lack of understanding the local customer, poor location or difficult access, management that does not know how to manage, and a lack of funds.

Growers

The nursery business is divided into greenhouse and outdoor growing environments. Outdoor plots used for growing plants, shrubs, or trees are essentially farms. A background in agriculture is helpful and some training is essential. Unless you have experienced a drought, bad markets, plant disease, and other realities of the grower's life, running a nursery is fraught with risk.

The first step is obtaining the land, although if you are already sure you want to run a nursery, you may already have that vital element in place. You will want to be sure the land is appropriately zoned. Check local regulations to see if agricultural zoning is the only viable option. You will also need to check if retail sales are possible on your property. Your state and county agricultural extension offices will have a number of resources and good advice for you, so be sure you establish a relationship with these experts. They are interested in helping nursery owners, and will be glad to talk with you about your plans. You will want a minimum of five to ten acres to start. Depending on the type of garden or nursery business you plan to operate, you may need parking space for customers and employees, sites for greenhouses and outdoor beds, and open areas where you will stock and grow trees and shrubs.

Location is key. If you are planning to grow wholesale, you can be located well off the beaten path since you will be shipping or trucking your products to retailers. If you are dealing only with landscaping professionals, and have no need to be accessible to the general public, you can be located far from population centers. But if you plan to sell to homeowners directly, you will need to be located within a reasonable driving distance from your customer base. It will also be helpful if your operation is near an interstate or has well-maintained roads — not gravel roads — leading to the retail center. After all, you will be competing with the retail stores that dot the suburbs of most American cities.

If you plan to operate as a grower and/or retailer, your business must comply with all applicable business laws and regulations. You need to be aware of basic retail zoning standards for your locale, such as building set-backs, lighting, signage, and so on. Any agricultural enterprise needs water. Its abundance and availability vary by region, but if you are in touch with your local agricultural extension service, you will know your local water situation and how to obtain sufficient amounts. If you are located in a remote area, you may need to drill a well or invest in and install irrigation systems to grow the plants you have in mind.

The regulation of fertilizers and pesticides is another area that you will address with your local extension agent. They will be able to provide complete information for your location regarding agricultural runoff. Following the rules will prevent you being fined or shut down by the Environmental Protection Agency (EPA). Being a good neighbor is essential for business success. It is important for the health of your community to maintain the purity of groundwater, rivers, lakes, and streams.

If you do not have a background or training in agriculture or farm operations, but still find the nursery-side of the business appealing, you may want to begin by buying products from other growers to retail to your customers. In other words, start by running a retail garden center. You may also want to take a job with a grower who operates a business similar to the type that interests you. What you hope to do is learn the business thoroughly before plunging into the risky unknown. Many successful landscapers and commercial nurseries focus their attention on pleasing retail customers and assisting them with growing advice, yard designs, and planting tasks. These nurseries purchase their stock from wholesale growers who are experts at the complex farming operations that profitable large-scale agriculture demands.

Products

As a nursery owner, plants are your products. Flowers, shrubs, and trees are grown in easy-to-plant, easy-to-maintain varieties, as well as exotic and expensive varieties that require extensive knowledge and horticultural skill. Think of it as geraniums versus orchids. Your level of experience and knowledge will determine your success in providing these products to your customers. You want to avoid a scatter-shot approach to your products and ser- vices. "We offer everything" may be a nice-sounding slogan, but for a small landscaping business, it does not work. It is far better to do one thing well than to do ten things poorly. Keep it simple.

The nursery business is seasonal in most areas of the United States. Spring is the prime season as homeowners and even apartment dwellers go in search for garden products. Your business must be set up to meet seasonal needs. This means you will need advance planning to ensure that a sufficient supply of whatever you choose to sell is available for purchase when demand is at its peak.

You have no doubt seen garden centers during the spring frenzy, with eager customers browsing flats of annuals, pointing and deciding what they would like to see growing on their spot of Mother Earth this year. Or perhaps they are considering a flower- ing tree that, in years to come, will provide shade in summer and sparkle in spring with a display of blooms. The nursery owner who offers these products must also be able to teach the plant buyer how to care for their new purchases. Providing one's cus- tomers with planting methods and tips on feeding, trimming, pest and disease prevention helps a good nursery become a great nursery. Many gardeners prefer to pay a little more for plants that are obviously well cared for (not wilted or shaggy) at nurseries where the owners and employees are well informed about their nursery stock and are eager to educate buyers.

Most retail outlets also offer bags of topsoil, fertilizer, grass seed, garden tools, pots, planters, and sometimes even paving stones and birdbaths. If you plan to operate such a retail business, you will require sources for all of these products. It is suggested that you maintain a wide selection of vendors so you have options when ordering, or when a particular item is in high demand.

Months before you open your business, take time to visit the types of retailers you would like to emulate and note their layouts, product lines, staff attitude, and knowledge. Identify and make notes of the small details that give the retail outlet its character — good or bad. Do you get a positive feeling when you walk in the door, or do you feel as though you are intruding on the sales person's time? If you have a question, does someone on staff have an answer? Do customers appear to be having a good time?

If you have the opportunity to talk with the owner, you may ask questions about the great service they provide, looking for hints that you might use when working with your future employees. You may also choose to make acquaintances with nurseries in cities far from your own. Befriending a distant retailer removes the fear of competition from the discussion. The competent nursery owner may feel flattered to give advice to a novice nursery proprietor from several states away.

As you assess any given garden center or retailer, check to see if customers appear to be wandering around on their own, or are they guided to what they want to see? Are the products assembled in a way that makes it easy to find grouped items such as flowers or shrubs? Do you enjoy the experience of being there, or are you waiting in a long line of impatient customers to get out? These are all important considerations as you decide what type of atmosphere you want to provide for your customers.

As with other aspects of the business world, there is no single "right way" to go into the retail plant business. You may want to start small and work up to a larger product line or retail outlet. You may begin your retail operation by offering flowers, shrubs, and trees to homeowners as part of their landscaping contracts, skipping the retail outlet altogether. This way, you can deal directly with growers and you will not have to concern yourself with acquiring land, planting and maintaining your products, or funding such things as greenhouses, tractors, special heaters, watering systems, or chemical tanks.

How to Make "Beautiful Work" Profitable

Wholesale nursery businesses are generally built on a handful of specific flowers, shrubs, or trees. It is difficult to make a profit when small numbers of many different varieties are being grown. Deciding to retail landscaping and gardening products, particularly if you plan to sell from a retail location, is a very different challenge from mowing lawns or designing and planting green spaces. If a nursery is your dream, the passion in your heart will give you extra energy to focus on the task. But, if you view running a nursery as an extension of indoor office work — dealing with vendors, purchasing, managing retail employees, and so on — then maybe you will be happier with one of the other outdoor service businesses, such as landscaping itself, or grooming yards. As a potential business owner, *you* get to decide.

Following is a list of critical factors you need to consider as you ponder the question of whether to enter the nursery business:

- Who will your customers be? Will you sell only to your own clients, or will you also supply products wholesale to other landscapers?

- Where will you grow or obtain your products?

- Do you want a retail outlet?

- What will your product line contain?

- Will you also sell non-plant items such as pots, planters, and paving stones?

- How will you ensure your plants are healthy and disease free?

- What will you do with leftover flowers and other plant products whose season is over?

- How will you ensure that you can meet seasonal demand?

- Where will you find trained staff?

- Can you make money doing this?

- What kind of competition do you face?

- How can you set your business apart from all of the other outlets for these products?

Competition from big box stores such as Wal-Mart or Home Depot can be strong. They have huge buying power, which means low prices for consumers — possibly lower than your cost of producing the same products. Unless you have a quality or product advantage, the huge national chains might be more competition than you want to take on.

Small, independent operations are always looking for ways to stand apart from their larger competitors. If you decide to compete for their business, visit some of the bigger outlets during the peak season and ask yourself where your advantage might be. Customer service may be one. Higher-end products might be another. Unique products, such as exotic plants or well-crafted garden accessories, may also draw customers to you. Some garden centers install coffee bars or conduct gardening and flower seminars for their customers. Some even set up pet centers so customers' dogs can run around while their owners check out the flora. Nothing is too wild in today's competitive environment. How much work and effort do you want to put into that part of your business and what is the payoff for you?

Most landscaping businesses will succeed if they offer planting services to customers who want more than just a mowed lawn, but running a nursery is a different focus. Think hard. What do you want to do?

Here the landscape architect expanded the arrival area by adding a brick walkway and plants to the edge of the driveway. Note how the plan invites the visitor to the front door.

This plan expands the basic stoop to an inviting outdoor area with stone walls and a brick patio and walkway.

Photos by Tom Hamm, Green Gardens, Inc.

Before photo: This home is on a sloping lot. The entry area is not defined or inviting.

*After photo: Landscape architect Tom Hamm and the team
at Green Gardens, Inc. have dramatically altered
the appearance and the feel of this home.*

SECTION THREE
Business Operations

Chapter Five

Planning for Success

Getting Started

You have made the decision. You are going into business for yourself as a landscaper, nursery owner, lawn service provider, or maybe all three. The next step is to prepare a business plan. You know where you want to go; now you must propose how to get there. This plan is your map. If you were traveling from Baltimore to Denver, you would not just head west and hope you run into Denver. You would look at a map and plan your trip. You would find your route number and have a schedule of where you want to be at various times on your journey. It is no different with your business. This is the key to your future as a successful owner of an outdoor business. "I want to be rich" may be an attractive answer, but it is not a business plan.

In the previous section, you examined the options for landscaping, nursery operations, and yard maintenance. You know what kind of business you would like to run. You probably already have a picture in mind of what your entry point into this business will be. If you have chosen lawn maintenance, are you going to begin by collecting residential customers? Do you plan on being aggressive and going after a few commercial customers as well? If you are considering landscaping or a nursery operation, lay out your options. Outline what your company will look like during the first month — then the second, third, and so on. Draft a one-year vision for your business, then a vision for two or three years out.

Stay as close to reality as you can, while remaining positive about your potential. Unless you already have a background in this field, it is not realistic to assume you will be a big player right away. It is realistic to assume that you can:

1. Survey your market

2. Analyze the potential for business

3. Learn what your competitors are charging

4. Determine what equipment you will need and how much it costs

5. Forecast your business expenses

6. Determine your personal financial needs (how much you need from this business to pay your own bills)

Business Planning

Here is the step-by-step process you will need to get your business going:

1. *Organize.* Ask yourself, what is your business all about? Write down a short, clear mission statement. For example, "Lance's Lawns offers high-quality lawn and garden care to residential and commercials customers. Our customer service is the best in the business. We stick by our word."

This is a broad statement, giving you latitude in determining the kinds of services and products you can eventually offer, but it also commits you to high business standards.

2. *Define*. What specific services will you offer right away? Write down if you will specialize in lawn mowing, edging, driveway cleaning, mulching, trimming, or if you will engage in more extensive landscaping services. If you are operating a nursery, describe what types of products you will grow and sell.

3. *Ownership*. Who owns the business? Only you, or do you have partners?

4. *Structure*. What is your business structure? Are you a sole proprietorship, an S corporation, or a limited liability company (LLC)? Structure types are discussed later in this chapter. Business consultants suggest that you do not operate your business as an individual or proprietorship because of liability and other risks.

5. *Credibility*. If you are going to borrow money to get your business going, you will need to write out a complete background report on yourself, explaining how and why you are qualified to operate this business successfully.

6. *Forecast*. What are your long-range plans for the business? Will you eventually offer walkways, ponds, stone walls, or commercial landscape development? When and how do you plan to do that?

7. *Research*. What is your market? Have you surveyed the market in your area so you know what the demand is and how much customers are willing to pay for such services?

Hint: If you have a lawn care company doing your own lawn, how much are you paying? What do your neighbors pay? Call a couple of real estate agents and ask them what the going rate is for typical residential yards. Maybe they have some thoughts about commercial jobs as well.

8. *Competition.* Who are your competitors? Is there one company that comes to mind when you think about landscaping services? Market impact is also known as "footprint." Does anyone have a big footprint in your area? Check the yellow pages to see who has invested in large advertisements. Go online to search for landscape companies in your area. Call them and learn if they will give you free estimates. The more information you can get during your planning phase, the better. Remember, it helps to know all you can find out about their pricing structure, and to get a feel for the people who work for them.

9. *Marketing.* What type of marketing will you do? If you have a business phone you will automatically be listed in the yellow pages. However, display ads cost extra. Think carefully before investing in a large display ad to start. A well-designed flyer may work better, either mailed or dropped on doorsteps in your target neighborhoods. Visit your printer to have business cards designed and printed. Join professional organizations such as builders and real estate associations, and business groups such as Business Network International and the Chamber of Commerce.

10. *Pricing.* How will you determine what you will charge for your services? Again, the basic market research will help you learn pricing for each of your services. Do not

assume you must be the cheapest guy in town. Playing the price game can be the road to failure. Know your costs and work with a reasonable margin. More details on how to price your services are found in Chapter 8.

11. *Equipment.* What will you need and how much does it cost? We will discuss equipment in Chapter 11.

12. *Vehicle.* Let us assume you will need only one in the beginning. You will probably need a full-size pickup, not necessarily new, and possibly a trailer to haul your equipment.

You must list all startup costs, including equipment, vehicles, tools, and other hard, capital expenses. You may need to rent a storage space for these things. Then, list marketing and advertising expenses, along with all other budget items for the first 6 to 12 months.

You also must forecast business income. How many customers do you think you can handle? Be realistic. You personally will not be able to cut 40 lawns a day. If you plan to hire someone, you must add that person's costs to your numbers. You may want to hold off on hiring anyone until you are situated. Slow and steady growth is preferable to a large financial commitment in a new business.

Before photo: This is a typical front yard.

After photo: Note how dramatic this same yard appears with terracing and professional landscaping.
Photos by Tom Hamm, Green Gardens, Inc.

Business plan checklist

Check these off as you complete each task.

Description of Your Business

	To Do	Done
What business structure will you use?	____	____
What is your company's name?	____	____
What services will you offer?	____	____

Marketing

What is your potential customer base?	____	____
How will you reach them?	____	____
Who are your major competitors?	____	____

Finances

How much money will you need to begin?	____	____
Where will you get it?	____	____
What are your financial projections?	____	____

Management

Who will run your company? ____ ____

Who is responsible for its success or failure? ____ ____

Who ultimately takes care of customers? ____ ____

The four major categories above are what the Small Business Administration (SBA) calls "distinct sections" of a business plan. We detail them later in Chapter 5.

Here are two examples of creative uses of lawn space.

Becoming a Small Business

A small business is a company with fewer than 500 employees. You will be joining more than 26 million other small businesses in the United States, according to the Small Business Administration. Small companies represent 99.7 percent of *all* employer firms in the country and contribute more than 45 percent of the total U.S. private payroll. More than half are home-based. Franchises make up two percent.

Of those 26 million small U.S. businesses, the SBA states that 649,700 new companies first opened for business in 2006. During the same period, 564,900 of the 26 million total closed shop. However, two-thirds of newly opened companies remain in business after two years and 44 percent after four years. The odds are with startups. Just keep in mind that virtually every one of the companies that survive do so because the owners are working hard and care about their company.

Basic business structures

Your state's business Web site may be the best place to start, but here is a brief description of business structures you might consider.

Sole proprietorship

This is the simplest, cheapest way to go into business. As a sole proprietor, you set up shop as yourself: *"Hi, I am Lance and I cut lawns."* Under this structure, the owner is personally liable for all business debts and other potential liabilities. You will be driving a truck, hauling equipment, and working in other people's yards and businesses. You may have other people working for you. If you or your employees cause damage or injury, your assets are seriously exposed. Many jurisdictions assume that sole proprietors will operate under their names. If you chose this form of business and are not going to use your name, you will likely be required to file the business name as a DBA (short for "doing business as") and may need state or municipal approval. As with all decisions regarding business structure, talk to an attorney who specializes in small business issues. He or she will be familiar with the laws and regulations you will be subject to and can advise you on ways to protect yourself.

Partnerships

This is similar to the sole proprietorship but involves more than one person. Profits, losses, and liabilities are shared. Management also may be shared. Naming the company is the same as the sole proprietorship, and may require the filing of a DBA. One caution here: Be sure you like your partner. If you choose to go into business with your best friend, realize the risk that doing business together could undermine or destroy your friendship. If you are considering a partnership, ask your partner if you can each be responsible for separate duties to avoid conflict.

A partnership may be a good idea if you do not feel strongly about running everything exactly your way. If you like being part of a team, you and your partner may find the shared experience of running a business a positive aspect of the work.

Be sure you have an attorney (you and your partner may wish to have separate attorneys) to set up the agreements that will cover what happens if you have a falling out, if one of you passes away, or if other contingencies occur.

Limited liability company (LLC)

This is more formal than the two structures outlined above, but not as formal as corporations. An LLC has advantages that limit your personal liability and offers certain tax benefits. You probably will have to file your LLC's name with the secretary of state, along with other documents. You will want to have an attorney involved in any of the business structures that go beyond a sole proprietorship.

C corporation

This is the most expensive and complicated way to go into business. You will be creating a legal entity separate from you and any others who may be involved. Some states require more paperwork, licensing, and taxes. For example, the corporation's profits will be taxed at the corporate level, and again when they are distributed to shareholders. Your accounting bill may be higher if you choose this structure; so will your legal bills. You also will have to issue stock certificates, hold annual meetings, elect officers, and all of the other formalities associated with corporations.

S corporation (sub chapter S)

This is similar to the C corporation, but it offers tax benefits to the owners. It will be taxed like a partnership, meaning there is no double taxation. Profits flow directly to the shareholders and are taxed as ordinary income. You are not required to have multiple shareholders. You can be the only one.

Again, discuss these issues with an attorney who specializes in small business matters. Also, find a reputable, certified public accountant (CPA) who specializes in small businesses. Talk to other small-business owners for referrals. Do not use your brother-in-law who took a tax course two years ago. A competent attorney and CPA will cost some money up-front, but are worth their expertise.

After you have made these decisions, you must meet your state and local requirements for conducting a legal business and obtain the necessary licenses, tax certificates, and other legalities of being in business. You must obtain a federal tax number, under which you will conduct your business and address tax issues such as payrolls and Federal Insurance Contributions Act (FICA). FICA is mandated by the federal government, and requires a portion of employers and employees paychecks to go towards funding Social Security and Medicare. Your federal tax number is easy to obtain, often with just a phone call. Be prepared to tell the person on the other end all the details of your business. This is another topic to discuss with your lawyer and accountant.

Once you have determined a structure for your enterprise, put a business plan together. For this example, we will call your company "Lance's Lawn Care and Nursery."

Parts of Your Business Plan

Essential elements:

1. Executive summary

2. Market analysis

3. Company description

4. Organization and management

5. Marketing and sales management

6. Services and products to be offered

7. Financials

8. Funding requests (if asking for loan)

We will make some assumptions as we work through this example plan, such as your structure, financials, equipment needs, and so on. Your specific plan must reflect your needs, marketing conditions, funding, and the advice you receive from your attorney and accountant.

Executive summary

Lance's Lawn Care and Nursery is a residential and commercial landscaping service offering basic-to-advanced lawn services, gardening, and landscape design to homeowners, property managers, and developers. Lance's Lawn Care and Nursery will target upper-income homeowners and upscale commercial areas, which need and can afford quality services of this nature. Real estate prices in this area have remained strong, despite the turn-out in other sections of the country, and demand remains high, thus offering growth opportunities.

Lance's Lawn Care and Nursery will begin as a limited liability company, LLC, owned entirely by Lance Lingering. Lance has worked as a lawn care and gardening specialist for the past eight years, as supervisor for Bob's Yards and Patios, and more recently as a master nursery supervisor at Elaine's Plants and Patios. Lance is a certified lawn maintenance quality-control specialist.

Lance's will open for business at the beginning of the region's lawn care season, which typically runs for seven months — April through October. During that time, Lance will hire one part-time helper to work up to 20 hours per week. Lance estimates his own workweek at 60 to 80 hours. If business warrants, Lance will hire a second, part-time worker.

Lance forecasts initial business at 20 to 30 residential customers requiring weekly yard maintenance, plus spring and fall services such as cleanup, mulching, and trimming. The average lawn maintenance fee will be $50, with some being higher or lower depending on yard size and services required. Spring and fall services will be in the $100 to $300 range. Anticipated monthly revenues during the first season from residential customers are expected to be $6,000, plus an additional $2,000 to $3,000 per month in April, May, and October from yard cleanup and preparation. We do not anticipate significant commercial contracts during the first season of business; however, we will market aggressively for commercial work for the following season, using the first year as a period of development and networking. Our first-year revenues are forecast at $49,500.

The above numbers are imaginary, but you get the idea. The summary explains the thinking that justifies the company and its future.

Market analysis

Lance's service area has experienced strong, sustained growth in population and property values over the past decade, even during recent setbacks in the real estate industry nationally. The growth of upper-income homes has been pronounced in communities with large lots. These homeowners a) have the financial resources to pay for first-class landscaping and b) little desire to do this type of work themselves. County planners expect more than 300 such homes to be sold and occupied in the coming 12 months, adding to the more than 1,000 such homes now occupied. Lance will target all of these residences so our estimate of 30 customers is modest. We expect to exceed that number quickly.

In addition, several retirement communities are under construction and Lance will market to the developers and management companies that oversee landscaping and maintenance. Lance has joined several professional groups that network decision makers in this segment.

Again, the idea here is to explain the market you intend to pursue.

Company description

Here you will formally explain the business structure you have selected. You are, for the purpose of this example, a limited liability corporation, LLC. In your specific case, you may elect something else. In this portion of your business plan, you would explain it, stating your officers, managers, and so on.

Organization and management

This is where you will be specific about how your company will be operated. Lance will be owner and general manager. If he plans to hire his wife or sister to do some daily bookkeeping, mention it here. If Lance's office will be at home, list it here. Where will equipment be stored? Will Lance need a storage facility? Be specific. Personnel and sales goals can also be mentioned here, and will be expanded upon later in this plan.

Marketing and sales management

Lance's Lawn Care and Nursery, LLC, will rely primarily on door-to-door marketing during its first quarter. We will distribute fliers at each home in our target area once a week for four weeks, approximately 4,000 fliers during the first month of operation. Each home will receive the flier at least twice. Two of our target communities permit solicitors to knock on doors, and Lance will personally knock on these doors on Saturday mornings for two hours each week to help him establish personal contact with potential customers and to offer on-the-spot consultations and estimates to build the initial customer base. Lance's initial marketing will focus on spring cleanup special offers.

Lance will also pass out business cards to developers, property managers, and other potential commercial customers, establishing potential relationships in the commercial arena.

This is where the plan meets the real world. Think this through and understand that this is the key part of your plan to make your business successful. All of your research and planning will focus on sales and marketing. Explain an entire year's worth of market planning — canvassing, networking, yellow pages, professional organizations, and any other advertising you plan to use.

Do not expect miracles from your marketing. Fliers generate 1 to 2 percent responses. Out of every 100 fliers you put out, you will get one or two calls. You should close more than half of these responses. The response rate goes up with frequency. Each time a potential customer sees your flier, the higher the likelihood that person will respond. Everything you do will add up to a total marketing strategy that will bring customers to your business.

Services and products

Here you expand on what you will do for your customers — lawn care, patios, walkways, tree trimming, and so on. If you live in an area with a short lawn season and a long, snowy winter, you may want to provide snow removal in the cold months. You need to determine how much income you can project for your services given the number of customers you can realistically anticipate in your first six months or year.

All of your services must be researched. You need to be aware of your competition, their prices, and the market. Do you plan to operate a nursery to sell plants and related products to the general public, in addition to landscaping or yard maintenance? If so, you will need a separate business plan for that, including a commercial site, permits, and products.

Services and Products Checklist

Service	Yes	No	Future
Yard work	____	____	____
Landscaping	____	____	____
Garden preparation/cleanup	____	____	____
Summer garden maintenance	____	____	____
Stump removal	____	____	____
Tree/bush trimming	____	____	____
Winter maintenance	____	____	____
Landscape design	____	____	____

Products

	Yes	No	Future
Walkways	____	____	____
Patios	____	____	____
Decks	____	____	____
Plants	____	____	____
Trees	____	____	____

Chemicals

	Yes	No	Future
Fertilizers	____	____	____
Pesticides	____	____	____

Note: Chemical handling is subject to federal, state, and local laws, licensing, certificates, and other conditions. Occupational Safety regulations also apply. Before you spread any fertilizers or pesticides as a commercial landscaper, you must meet these requirements. The Environmental Protection Agency (**www.epa.gov**) and the Occupational Safety and Health Administration (**www.osha.gov**) have more information, as does your state government Web site.

List any other products and services you plan to offer, now or in the future.

_____

_____

Financials

Here is where you make your financial projections for your first three years. These are estimates based on solid information and market conditions but, as with all business activities, nothing is guaranteed. Nevertheless, this is a financial blueprint.

First, make a column of all of the services you plan to offer and forecast sales for them.

Service	2008	2009	2010
Yard work	$7,500	$10,000	$12,500
Lawn care	$42,000	$50,000	$55,000

Products	2008	2009	2010
Trees	$5,000	$6,500	$7,000
Flowers	—	—	—

List all of your services and products and what you reasonably expect them to bill.

Next, list your costs. These would include cost of goods (not equipment, which is a capital expense), rent, phone, marketing, insurance, fuel, equipment maintenance, and other costs of doing business.

Costs	2008	2009	2010
Storage rental	$8,000	$8,000	$8,000
Phone	$600	$625	$700
Insurance	$2,000	$2,100	$2,200
Ad/marketing	$5,000	$6,000	$8,000
Fuel	$1,800	$2,000	$2,000

It is important that you make a good faith effort at predicting your costs. Your actual expenses may be higher or lower than your initial projections so track your expenses monthly to allow for adjustments. For instance, you may increase or decrease your marketing expenses according to projected costs versus actual expenses.

Labor

Here is where you list your labor expenses. How much are you going to pay yourself and your part-time employee(s)? If you have employees, you must pay unemployment insurance, workers' compensation insurance, and possibly other fees, depending on your state's laws.

Startup costs

List here what you anticipate the cost of opening your business will be — equipment, vehicles, tools, trailers, fees, licenses, computer, software, and all of the other costs associated with starting a business. If you are planning a small lawn cutting and mulching operation for the first few months or a year, your expenses will be lower. On the other hand, if you want to begin as a full-service company offering a wide range of lawn care and nursery services, you will need substantial start-up capital.

You will need a vehicle to haul your equipment to job sites. A full-sized pickup truck is a reasonable option, although you may choose a van. Remember, these are work trucks — you will not want or need leather seats, heated drink holders, or a premium sound system. You will need a vehicle you can beat up, so stay away from anything that needs to be pampered. You may want to consider a used truck; something that is mechanically sound, physically acceptable, with low mileage, and low cost. Avoid purchasing a vehicle that has major dents or other cosmetic problems because your company's name will be on it and customers (and potential customers) will judge your company by the condition of you _____ does not mean it has to be spotless, but you do n_____ company associated with a beat-up wre_____nce and a quality image in ev_____

_____ area dealer lots, then price _____thy cost difference between a _____odel. Larger, more-established _____olicy of replacing their vehicles _____k out for deals.

_____ nt such as mowers and tractors can also _____ ls such as shovels, rakes, hoes, hoses, and other co_____ mplements should be purchased new and at top grade. You _____ not want to get bargain tools for a professional landscaping business, as they will not hold up to the heavy-duty work you will be doing.

Funding requests

If you are going to borrow the money needed to start the business, you must provide a detailed financial statement in addition to the information you already have in your business plan. This is the same information you would provide for any substantial loan from a bank or other financial institution. You must provide assurance that you can and will pay back the loan and offer a form of security. This might be your home or other assets such as savings, stocks, or real estate. Your business and its assets will be part of the security package. We will cover more details about funding your business in Chapter 7.

If you are purchasing a franchise, you likely will not be able to use the franchise as collateral because franchisors typically retain sole rights to award franchises, and therefore may not honor any claims against the franchise. This means if you put your business up as collateral and default on the loan, the lender cannot take over your franchise, so it is useless as collateral.

If you are considering the purchase of a landscaping or lawn service franchise, the law requires that the franchisor provide you with a detailed report explaining every aspect of the business. This is a requirement of the Federal Trade Commission (FTC), which advises all prospective franchisees to read these reports carefully. A meticulous review will protect yourself and your investment. It is suggested that you employ a lawyer or CPA who is aware of FTC regulations to double-check these documents for potential problems.

You may have noticed the words "lawyer" and "accountant" again. As stressed earlier, these two professionals can save you from trouble and losing money. One more option many startup companies have used, especially in the past: credit cards. If you have good personal credit and a high enough limit, you may be able to borrow the money from yourself. Be wary of high interest rates, and be sure you will be able to pay the monthly fees. Talk to your accountant and your banker about loan details. If you lend money to your company, you may be entitled to interest on the loan, as well as repayment.

Insurance

Insurance is a necessary expense, and in some jurisdictions, an absolute requirement for doing business. No matter how careful you are accidents will happen so insurance is your protection.

As the owner of a landscaping business you have many assets to protect, the most important of which is the business itself. Unless a corporate shield protects you, your personal assets are also at risk and could be lost in a lawsuit if you do not have the proper insurance protections.

Types of insurance

Insurance is not a one-size-fits-all solution. Laws vary by state, so some states will have higher premiums, based on a number of factors, including the number of claims filed overall. If you are licensed to use chemicals, you may find that your insurance costs for that category of service are higher than for other services you provide. Insurance companies may consider lawn chemicals as a higher risk because misuse or accidents with them could lead to serious claims by people who were affected.

A prospective insurer will examine the list of services you provide, your vehicle(s), equipment, and the number of employees you have on the payroll to help determine your premiums. These basic business facts will also help you determine what types of insurance you need. Ask yourself "What can I afford to lose?" in the event of a catastrophic claim by a customer, subcontractor, or vendor.

Environmental damage is another serious risk for landscaping businesses. If a large canister of pesticides overturns, polluting a stream, your business may face civil suits and hefty government fines. Defense attorneys and court actions are expensive. You do not want to find yourself trying to scrape up the money to cover such extraordinary costs.

Many states have minimum business insurance standards. A description of some common types of insurance follows:

Comprehensive general liability insurance

General liability insurance may be required in your state. This type of insurance will cover your business against unexpected accidents and injuries. Review the policy for exclusions that might leave you vulnerable to exposure under certain circumstances. Read the fine print — do not ignore it or skim over it. For example, if your policy excludes damage caused by drunken employees, the insurance company may not help you if an inebriated employee loses control of your company truck.

Know what you need and what coverage an insurance company is providing. Talk to a number of providers. Better yet, ask other business owners for referrals to reputable insurance brokers who deal with a range of insurance companies. He or she will shop around for the coverage you need at the lowest cost. The most important part of this process is obtaining the proper coverage. A lower premium is not worth much if you find yourself without the insurance protection you need.

How much liability coverage is enough? $1 million sounds like a lot, but in today's world that amount may not be enough. $2 million is probably a minimum; $3 million is safer. If you can afford it, go higher. You will find that insurance companies price this type of insurance reasonably, assuming you do not have a history of claims and judgments, and premiums are not based on a dollar-for-dollar fee schedule. $2 million in coverage is less than twice the cost of $1 million, and so on. An insurance broker who specializes in small business coverage can help you determine what you need. Be honest with him or her and do not mislead them, or yourself, about what you will be doing in your business — whether it is outlining the services you provide, or the products you are offering. Ask questions, write down the coverage you need and any promises regarding coverage from the provider or the broker, and check these items against the actual insurance policy.

Bonding

If you already have general liability insurance, do you also need to have company and employees bonded? The answer is—sometimes, yes. Liability insurance covers accidental property damage or injury caused by you, the contractor, to your customer's property or people on the site, but it does not compensate for construction defects or poor workmanship. A surety bond is an agreement the contractor arranges with a bonding company, to pay awards to the consumer if the contractor is judged at fault, by arbitration or legal action, if a job is not completed to the customer's satisfaction. State laws differ but it is common for states to require contractors to carry surety bonds of a certain level, depending on their license category. Bonding is usually a requirement for jobs with the government or large commercial jobs.

Although it is expensive to carry both liability insurance and a surety bond, it helps attract and keep customers who understand that their property and investment will be protected, no matter what. Plus, you can then charge premium rates, because not every person with an outdoor service business carries this coverage. You can find a bond provider who works with businesses in your state at the National Association of Surety Bond Producers: **www.nasbp.org/AM/Template.cfm?Section=Find_a_ Producer_in_your_State&Template=/CM/HTMLDisplay. cfm&ContentID=1844**

Employee bonding is a different matter. Employee dishonesty bonds are surety bonds that guarantee compensation if your employee steals property or is otherwise negligent on the job. You may want this coverage because, frankly, you never know what another person is thinking. Talk to your insurance agent to see if it is necessary.

Product liability insurance

Product liability insurance is a separate category that provides protection from problems arising from the products you sell. Patios may sink, walkways may crack and trip someone, or some other product could fail. Be sure your business is covered against this type of risk.

Workers' compensation insurance

Worker's Comp, as it is commonly called, is required in every state. However, the structure of the insurance varies by state. Private insurance companies offer this coverage based on the number of employees on the payroll, the roles each individual performs, and the type of business you are operating. However, some states require that such coverage be obtained from the state government or one of its agencies. This insurance pays medical expenses and lost wages for workers who are injured on the job. There are exclusions for certain categories, such as independent contractors and volunteers, but, again, check your state's laws. Business owners are generally exempt in most cases.

Home-Based business insurance

Home-based insurance will be required if you are working out of an office in your home. Homeowners' policies rarely cover business losses. If you are operating from your home or garage, check with your insurance agent to see if anything in your office is covered. The typical homeowner's policy specifically excludes home-based business losses, including equipment, theft, loss of data, and personal injury. Unfortunately, many companies that provide homeowner's insurance do not offer business coverage, so you may need to have two insurance companies covering different areas of your home.

Criminal insurance

Criminal insurance covers you in the event of an employee committing a crime. General liability insurance may not cover theft or other criminal acts by employees. If someone is on your payroll, you may be held responsible for his or her actions in a customer's home, including the yard. Should that person steal something, vandalize that home, or deliberately harm a resident, the homeowner will expect you to assume responsibility. This type of coverage can also protect you in the event of employee embezzlement. Depending on your general liability coverage, you may want to consider this category of insurance.

Surety bonds

Surety bonds are performance guarantees that fall under the insurance category. This is a way to assure a client or customer that your company will complete work as stated in a contract. Small customers, such as homeowners, probably will not ask for this guarantee (at least not in this form) but large commercial customers will want to know you have the financial resources to get the work done. If you have bid on a $1 million project that involves labor and material, you must have some way to pay your expenses, and cash flow for small businesses can be a deal breaker. Surety bonds (also called performance bonds) are available from insurance companies. If you cannot get such coverage on the commercial market, the Small Business Administration has a Surety Bond Program that may be available to you — but, as with all government programs, be prepared for paperwork.

Key man insurance

Key man insurance may be required by lenders who provide capital for businesses. This coverage applies to the person whose absence from the company would cause it to fail. Most likely, that person would be you or your partner. If you have borrowed money to start or operate your business, the lender may require such insurance as a guarantee of payment if anything were to happen to you.

Business interruption insurance

Business interruption insurance covers your expenses if you are shut down by fire, natural disaster, or other catastrophe. Landscaping businesses are not as vulnerable to this as other types of businesses, so look carefully at your other coverage. Assuming your equipment and vehicles are already covered, you may not want to duplicate coverage. Discuss this with your provider or broker.

Vehicle insurance

Vehicle insurance is the commercial version of the insurance you have on your private vehicle. The same price considerations apply: type of vehicle, history of claims, mileage, location, and drivers. If you have employees who will drive your vehicles, their driving records will be considered in the rate you pay, along with yours.

Insurance Review

Insurance is not an option — it is protection that is required both by law and good sense. There is no single standard for business insurance because laws, rates, and requirements vary by state.

At a minimum, you will need comprehensive general liability insurance, vehicle insurance, workers' compensation insurance, and probably home-based business insurance. You may also consider product liability and criminal insurance policies. Your lender may require key man insurance if you have borrowed money for your business.

Ask other small business owners in your area for referrals to a reputable business insurance broker and review your options and requirements with her or him to determine the best coverage for business and to find the best rates.

Have your insurance coverage in place before you mow your first lawn or provide any business service to customers.

Insurance Checklist

Type of Insurance	Mandatory? Y/N	Coverage/$	Cost/$
Comprehensive Liability	_____	_____	_____
Product Liability	_____	_____	_____
Workers' Compensation	_____	_____	_____
Home-Based Business	_____	_____	_____
Key Man	_____	_____	_____
Criminal	_____	_____	_____
Business Interruption	_____	_____	_____
Vehicle(s)	_____	_____	_____
Total Insurance Cost			_____

Other insurance options/needs:

_____

_____

CASE STUDY: ST. LOUIS LAWN CARE, TIM JENKERSON

St. Louis Lawn Care
3524 Glen Arbor Dr
St. Louis, MO 63125
314-974-5911
www.STLLawnCare.com

The roots of St. Louis Lawn Care go back to 1995, when Tim Jenkerson's father started a lawn care business in the off hours from his jobs as a police officer and a fireman. He started with a small commercial lawnmower and a little truck, and Jenkerson and his brother Nick helped him throughout high school and college.

At the time, the Internet was gaining popularity, and Jenkerson had a college friend who was involved in high-tech search engine optimization and Web sites. Jenkerson picked his friend's brain, did some research of his own, and built his dad a Web site. It brought in so much business that "he couldn't handle it," said Jenkerson.

Jenkerson graduated with an accounting degree and worked for a while in that field, but decided to put his phone number on the Web site to see if he could get some lawn care business for extra money. It worked so well that Jenkerson opened St. Louis Lawn Care. He and his father operated separately for a year, but recently combined the two businesses under the St. Louis Lawn Care name.

Jenkerson, his father (who remains a police officer), and his brother are all working partners in the business, which includes one full-time and two part-time employees. The business is home-based. Services include mowing, trimming, mulching, fertilizer applications (organic and standard), overseeding, sod, leaf removal, and snow plowing. They also perform light landscaping services and build retaining walls. Ninety percent of their business is residential, with ten percent commercial.

The Web site is their primary marketing tool. It features a lawn care blog, as well as a complete description of services. The company also offers a referral program that rewards residential customers who refer a friend with a free fertilizer application or grass cutting when their friend signs a yearly agreement. Annual contracts carry over year to year, unless a customer cancels.

They do their own equipment maintenance such as oil changes and blade sharpening, but if anything major goes wrong, they take it to a service shop. They have a couple backup mowers in place to use if one goes out.

CASE STUDY: ST. LOUIS LAWN CARE, TIM JENKERSON

"It's not super expensive to start a lawn business," Jenkerson said, "but there are startup costs with everything you do. I got lucky. Since my Dad had all the equipment, I just used his to start with, and then bought my own eventually."

What do new business people need to know? "It helps to know how the equipment operates, and lawn maintenance skills," he said. Jenkerson advises to cut grass 2' to 2.5' high in the cool season, then raise it up to 3'-3.5' in the summer. They price each lawn individually, factoring in both market price and time. "It's basically experience."

Chapter Six

Branding Your Business

Branding your business is primarily the process of creating a distinctive difference in the customer's mind — a specific perception that sets your business apart from others doing roughly the same thing. Branding incorporates the entire atmosphere of your business, from naming, logo design and the quality of the products you provide, to the level of excellence in the services you perform and your relationship with your customers. It even incorporates the way you interact with and support your community, through sponsoring kids' sports team uniforms, donating to charities, and the like. It all goes together.

Branding is no longer just for tangible products. Branding is for services like landscaping, plant nurseries and garden centers, and lawn maintenance as well.

You can think of your brand as the personality of your business. If you offer a strong, stable, dependable business personality or brand, potential customers will feel more confident in employing you, and in trusting you to follow through on your promises. If you are able to establish a branded position in your community —

if your business becomes *the name* that people recall when asked about landscaping, yard work, or the nursery business — then you will receive recommendations even from people who have never used your services. This is a most-desirable situation. Although branding can be driven by a catchy name, a well-designed logo, and persistent, memorable advertising and marketing efforts, the value of the brand comes down to the quality you deliver.

The simple reality of business is that you will need to offer customers something that others cannot or will not offer. That is the core of the brand you are hoping to create.

One good way to begin analyzing branding is to search for the most up-to-date information available for your field, both online and off. Subscribe to newsletters, magazines, news services, forums, chat rooms, Web sites, and follow the links we list in the bibliography. Thanks to the Internet, you have much greater access to free information by signing up for newsletter mailing lists on Web sites related to landscaping.

When you visit a successful landscaping business Web site, note how they position themselves, the kind of information they offer, the words they use to present their business to customers. You may make a few phone calls to these companies yourself, asking innocent questions to see how the person who answers the phone responds to a stranger's call. Examine everything, from the visual impression and pricing to products and services. Once you have examined the leading competitors in your community you will be able to consider the most reasonable position you can take to set yourself apart from them.

A brand can benefit the operation of your business by:

- Building strong customer loyalty

- Bringing more credibility to any project

- Delivering any company message fast and effectively

- Hitting an emotional level with people

- Separating yourself and your business from the competition

- Positioning a focused message in both the heart and mind of your target market

- Bringing consistency to your marketing promotions and campaigns

As a small business owner, it may seem that "branding" your business or yourself may simply be a "slick" advertising move. However, branding your small business is more about positioning your business and yourself in a positive light so your target market can see your business is the best choice above the others. When you build a business brand it is not only about what you do but also about the benefits your customer will receive from you that they would not receive from another company. Your goal is to keep your customers coming back and to renew your contracts with them year after year.

A brand helps you to organize the full range of your marketing and advertising strategies. It will convey what you stand for and who you are. An effective brand will encompass the whole business, and will include a special logo that will be everywhere in the business: on stationery, cards, packaging, signs, and more. This brand also will fit right in the pricing of the services or products, customer services, and your business's guarantees.

Creating an Effective Brand

How do you go about creating a winning brand that will help customers identify your business with everything that will make them feel comfortable and confident with you? Here are a few suggestions to get you started:

- Identify your personal and business values. Begin to construct this by listing both personal and business values (honesty, quality, and so on). Then create a "value statement" for your business based on this list. Keep it short. The more condensed your value statement is, the easier it will be for you to recall. In addition, the condensed value statement may be the perfect phrase to use as an advertising tag line that will appear on your marketing materials.

- Create a mission statement. A mission statement lays out the purpose underlying your work. For example, you may want to define your landscaping mission as "Providing color and beauty for homeowners and builders throughout the Tristate area while maintaining grounds all year round." A good mission statement is meaningful, but still short enough to remember.

- Create a vision statement. A good vision statement will specify how you will know when you have achieved the goal of your mission statement. Setting targets for yourself, and then continually striving to meet them, helps keep you working smarter and remain innovative as new possibilities open up.

- Identify your starting point. Where are you right now in relation to where you want to be? Write down some of the steps you already know are necessary to make your business dreams become real.

- Describe your market. Understanding who you want to reach with branding is critical, since choices of advertising, marketing, and other types of publicity will vary depending on the target market(s) you select.

- Create a positioning statement. Positioning is your attempt to control the image of the business your customer will see. What is the impression you hope to make in the mind of your ideal customer? In your community, will you aim to be the lowest-cost provider? The top-quality provider? The most friendly, reliable provider?

Naming your business

Ideally, the name of your business captures its essence. There are pros and cons for using your name for your business. When you share your name and identity with your company, you create a personal connection with your clients and with your target market. You also use your personal reputation and community image to help build up your business.

The naming process takes place after you have determined the structure of the business you are proposing. You will want to be sure the name you select is legal and accurately reflects what your business does. Verify that no other business in your area shares the name you are considering. You may have to file your name with your state or local government for approval. You may not legally call yourself "Lance's Licensed Lawn Care" if you do not have a license.

If you purchase a franchise, you will not be allowed to incorporate under the franchisor's name. Say you purchased a "Lance's Lawn" franchise. You cannot legally incorporate under that name because Lance has already done that. You must incorporate under, say, Bob's Lawns, Inc., DBA Lance's Lawns of Glendale.

Avoid long, hard-to-remember names. You may brainstorm business name ideas with friends, business advisors, or others. Think not only of how the name will sound when you answer the phone, but how it will look on a flyer or other advertising. Reserve the URL or Web address of your Web site as soon as you choose a business name, even if you do not plan to set the Web site up for a few months. Also, you might want to check the availability of selected Web addresses before you settle on a name.

While calling your business by the owner's name is a common approach, "Joe's Lawn Care" is descriptive but boring. You may want to go beyond the obvious. If so, it is fine to explore your creativity. If you are unsure how come up with a creative name, get out the yellow pages and look at the wide variety of names for hair salons, restaurants, or other businesses. Pick out your favorites, and then try to understand why they appeal to you. Ask outsiders — friends, relatives, professional advisors — what they think of your ideas, and if they have suggestions. You want to avoid being too "cute" or unprofessional, while still being memorable.

Develop your logo

The logo is a visual symbol of your business and your brand. There are many different considerations to keep in mind when choosing a logo or having one designed for you. You will probably want to keep it graphically simple, so it can be enlarged or made smaller, yet remain easily recognizable. A professional graphic designer may be helpful in preparing the symbol for use in multiple formats. It should look as good on a billboard as it does on your truck, an invoice statement, or your business cards.

You will also want to think ahead to the cost of reproducing your logo. Ideally it will look good in black and white as well as in color, because color printing costs more and you may want to conserve costs at some point. If it renders well in blacks and grays, it will deliver that much more punch when you can afford to print it in color.

The combined effect of your values statement, mission statement, vision and position statement, plus your definition of market, your business name, and your logo will become, over time, the foundation of your brand. Your unique "business personality" will be presented to the target market through business cards, fliers, brochures, online ad mediums, the yellow pages, and possibly newspaper, radio, or TV advertising. If you develop unified themes and are consistent in presenting your business message and image, your brand will grow with you as your customer list increases. People will know who you are and what you represent. That consistent, positive message will greatly increase your chances for profits and long-term success.

Regional design will provide a distinctive appearance, such as this Southwestern landscape.

CASE STUDY: GREEN MAN ENVIROSCAPING, EVERETT A. WARREN

440 Acorn Drive
Lehighton, PA 18235
610-442-7964
www.greenmanenvy.com

Everett A. Warren was still working as a computer programmer when the economy started to tank. "With programming jobs going to India, I decided to do something else. Ever since I was a kid, I was into the idea of natural landscaping," he says. "The environmentally-safe products are a little tougher to go with, but it was important to come up with something that differentiates me from the other landscapers and maintenance crews out there," he said. "It was something I could feel good about."

Warren operates his business as an LLC, and currently employs himself and one full-time employee. His 17-year-old son works part-time. They have done a lot of recent work for the non-profit Lehigh Gap Nature Center, placing 100' by 100' deer exclosures on a mountainside that was heavily damaged by the a nearby zinc plant. Now the mountainside is part of a Superfund hazardous waste site, and it is being seeded with native prairie grasses and wildflowers.

No one knows yet how well the plants will survive on soil that contains up to eight percent zinc. Researchers want the exclosures in place to evaluate deer pressure on the new seedlings and grasses. Warren got work with the non-profit partly due to relationships he built as a volunteer there, both before and after he started his landscaping company. "I give them a day [every] month for free," he said. "I do plowing on the access road for them in winter, brush cutting and string trimming in summer. They pay the fuel, but I donate the labor.

CASE STUDY: GREEN MAN ENVIROSCAPING, EVERETT A. WARREN

It shows we are environmentally-friendly as a company — putting your money where your mouth is."

Although Warren expected his business to be more dependent on lawn maintenance, it is not turning out that way. His natural design/build concepts attract more customers. "I really can't compete with a kid with no insurance, and a lawnmower in the back of a pickup truck," said Warren. "I also can't compete with a lawn maintenance company that has crews and z-turn mowers. They can take care of a yard a lot quicker than I can." Instead, Warren is active in new lawn installations, using grass seed approved for organic applications, and organic materials to help it grow. "We bring in topsoil, and add products like Jonathan Green's KickStart™ to add nutrients to the soil and build it back up again." He also installs natural gardens with native and other non-invasive plants. "We can make even a small space look like a wild place." He does not presently apply herbicides, which require special licensing and permits.

The best piece of advice Warren offers someone going into the business is to be sure to have enough capital. While Warren had enough capital to do what he did the first year, it did not cover as much as he originally planned. "I started with a Deere Brushmower ™ fitted with attachments, like a snow blower, a small plow, and a 42-inch lawn deck. The 42–inch lawn deck is big enough for an
acre property." A desk is still on the company wish list, so he does most of his office work in the cab of his truck. His next big equipment purchase will be a Boxer Mini-Skid™ by Compact Power. "It doesn't have a cab, but it has tracks, and a little platform you stand on, an auger and 50 different available attachments," he said.

Despite the challenges of starting a company during an economic slump, Warren enjoys many personal benefits. "Sitting in a cubicle, I was getting sick frequently, got overweight, had high blood pressure and allergies. Now I'm outside all the time, and I don't have those problems anymore."

Chapter Seven

Funding Your Business

If you have all the money you need to start your business, you can skip this section for now. But, sooner or later, you may need to find outside sources of funding to purchase equipment or supply working capital, among other possibilities. The US Small Business Administration suggests asking the following questions before seeking financial assistance:

- Do you need more capital or can you manage existing cash flow more effectively?

- How do you define your need? Do you need money to expand or as a cushion against risk?

- How urgent is your need? You can obtain the best terms when you anticipate your needs rather than looking for money under pressure.

- How great are your risks? All businesses carry risks, and the degree of risk will affect cost and available financing alternatives.

- In what state of development is the business? Needs are most critical during transitional stages.

- For what purposes will the capital be used? Any lender will require that capital be requested for very specific needs.

- What is the state of your industry? Depressed, stable, or growth conditions require different approaches to money needs and sources. Businesses that prosper while others are in decline will often receive better funding terms.

- Is your business seasonal or cyclical? Seasonal needs for financing generally are short term.

- How strong is your management team? Management is the most important element assessed by money sources.

- Perhaps most importantly, how does your need for financing mesh with your business plan? If you do not have a business plan, make writing one your first priority. All capital sources will want to see your business plan for the start-up and growth of your business.

Financing Options

You may want to consider the two types of financing options: debt or equity. You will want to compare the amount of money you have borrowed (debt) with your personal financial investment (equity). This calculation is called the debt-to-equity ratio; in other words, the comparison between the amount of money you have borrowed and your personal financial investment in your business. The more money you have invested personally in your start-up business, the easier it is to attract financing later on.

If your business has a high ratio of equity to debt, you should probably apply for a bank loan. However, if your business is already deeply in debt, you should probably seek to increase your ownership capital (equity investment).

Debt financing

There are many sources for debt financing: banks, savings and loans, commercial finance companies, and the U.S. Small Business Administration (SBA) are the most common. In recent years state and local governments have developed many programs to encourage the growth of small businesses in recognition of their positive effects on the economy. Family members, friends, and former associates are all potential sources, especially when capital requirements are smaller.

Traditionally, banks have been the major source of small business funding. Their principal role has been as a short-term lender offering demand loans, seasonal lines of credit, and single-purpose loans for machinery and equipment. Banks generally have been reluctant to offer long-term loans to small businesses. The SBA guaranteed lending program encourages banks and non-bank lenders to make long-term loans to small businesses by reducing their risk and leveraging the funds they have available. The SBA's programs have been an integral part of the success stories of thousands of businesses nationally.

Lines of credit

A line of credit loan is designed to provide short-term funds to a company to maintain a positive cash flow. Then, as funds are generated later in the business cycle, the loan is repaid. Most commercial banks offer a revolving line of credit when a fixed amount is available.

In addition to equity considerations, lenders commonly require the borrower's personal guarantees in case of default. This requirement provides a serious, incentive for the business owner to attend to business details and ensure loan repayment. For most borrowers this is a burden, but also a necessity.

Equity financing

Most small or growth-stage businesses use limited equity financing. As with debt financing, additional equity often comes from non-professional investors such as friends, relatives, employees, or even customers. You may put your home or other assets up for collateral, or use money obtained through a home-equity loan to underwrite certain business expenses. Discuss this sort of transaction with your accountant before you make a decision to do this, because you are literally mortgaging your home to support the enterprise. If you can see a way that the money will be readily paid back, it may be a safe way to go. If in reality you are pouring cash from your home into a serious business problem, alternatives such as soliciting an investment from a wealthy friend or family member may be a wiser decision. However, this person may insist on a stake in your company or other influence in return for the investment.

There are special sources of funding for different catergories of business owners, such as minorities. Your banker may have knowledge of such sources, or you can contact your local Small Business Development Center (SBDC). Approximately 1,000 SBDCs have been formed and partially funded by the US Small Business Administration. The SBDCs link universities, state, and local governments. They are designed to assist new and existing business owners with free consultation and low-cost training in virtually every aspect of business operation, including finding funds to continue or expand.

The SBDC member programs assist more than one million businesses every year. A large number of these businesses are just getting off the ground, but the majority are existing businesses with concerns about handling transitions, stabilizing their operation, or planning for expansion. You can access the network of Small Business Development Centers to find your closest office on the Web at **http://sbdcnet.org/sbdcs-nationwide-12.php.**

Professional Advisors

For many business owners who are not involved in a partnership, one of the more frustrating aspects of being the boss is not having someone to bounce ideas off of, or to ask for help. The SBDC consultants, mentioned previously, are one avenue to outside advice. Remember that while they are there to serve your needs, they are also serving the needs of dozens or hundreds of other business owners too.

You will want to create a personal network of business advisors, including those with professional credentials. The sooner you can bring experts into your business team, the better for both you and your fledgling business. Be sure to include these professionals on your short list of necessary advisors:

- A certified accountant (CPA) or someone of equal ability in accounting. You will need this person for advice and to provide services on taxes (US, state, and local), loan terms, vehicle purchases — practically anything to do with money. A competent accountant can show you how to get the most profit for each dollar of income. He or she might even have good ideas on additional sources of income you could provide. If you do not know a good accountant whom you trust, get first-hand referrals from a successful business owner or banker.

- A capable business attorney. Build a relationship with a good business attorney so you always have someone knowledgeable on hand if you need to have someone go over a contract to look out for your special interests, if you need legal advice in hiring situations, or for advising on legal forms and requirements at your state and local level. You will want someone experienced. It is not good for you to be the guinea pig for a start-up attorney, even if you are running a start-up yourself.

- A business-banking expert from your primary business bank. You want a banker who is interested in the growth of your company, who is literally "banking" on your success. A good business banker can help you network with vendors, or even find new customers. Often the business banker has a deep reservoir of business knowledge that he or she would like to share with you, so ask questions.

- A solid business insurance agent or broker. A broker may be your wisest choice since, in theory at least, they check out several different insurance companies for you and recommend only what they believe is best. Look to a professional insurance advisor to help you analyze and prepare for your business risk.

Perhaps you do not want anything to do with certain aspects of your business, but you do not want to hire employees either. Whether it is weekly bookkeeping, or laying a stone walkway, if you do not feel comfortable or competent in performing a necessary business task, it is far better to find the right service to handle it than to neglect the job or mess it up. Use your professional advisors — banker, accountant, attorney — as a starting point to find the services that will help you get your worst jobs done right.

Money Management

Business success is directly connected to sound money management—keeping careful track of the amount of money that comes in, where it comes from, how much money goes out, and who receives it. Sound money management begins with knowing your costs. Ideally, you will calculate your best estimate of operating cost *before* you start your business, and build in regular re-evaluations to be sure your estimates are on the mark once your business is underway.

You will want to know your basic cost of doing business — the amount you need to meet just to remain solvent — *before* you add on products that customers are purchasing from you. If that number is $5,000, and there are 30 days in a month, you must make an average of $167 for each day of the month just to pay your basic expenses. In other words, you do not make any money until you exceed that amount.

Start this process by estimating what it costs you to be in business for one month. Add up fixed costs, such as rent, phones, truck payments, ongoing marketing expenses, and the costs of your equipment spread out over their expected working life. For instance, if your mower costs $1,000 and you expect it to last three eight-month seasons, the mower cost is $41 per month. You can expand that to a 12-month season if you like, for a monthly cost of $28. Do not forget to add in the monthly cost of gas, oil, blades, and general maintenance. Truck, trailer, and other vehicles will be accounted for in the same manner to arrive at their monthly costs.

You will also need to figure employee wages and benefits, and many other costs. An accountant may be able to give you a more detailed approach to determine your costs. That is another benefit of working with a professional expert. The point is to have a realistic method of determining costs so you will know how to factor them into your pricing. Your cost of doing business should always be borne by the customer, not your business.

Taxes

Taxes are a critical factor in sound money management. It is essential to maintain records of all sales and expenses, down to the last penny. The Internal Revenue Service (IRS) will want to see what came in and what went out, especially if your business is ever audited. Clear, up-to-date records show that you are a responsible taxpayer, and help avoid any suspicion of shady policies. Keep your company above board and financially transparent to the parties that have a legal right to see the numbers.

Also recognize that keeping accurate books is not a favor to the government. Your financial records are an ongoing map of your business's life. If you do not keep accurate and detailed numbers, you will not have any idea how your company is doing financially. You must have the numbers and understand them to know whether you are meeting your goals and have a decent profit margin.

You will want to make sure your federal, state, and local taxes are filed on a timely basis. In some places, you may be required to collect sales tax on products or services, and pay it to the governing body periodically. Verify these requirements by contacting your city or state tax department. They will tell you what licenses or tax filings are necessary, as well as the schedule and appropriate ways to file. Many taxing entities are converting to online tax filings for businesses. You will need to set up a special account on the related government Web site to use online filing and payment methods.

Controlling Costs

Controlling costs is the most challenging aspect of business. You are not in business as entertainment or just to occupy your time. You are in business to make money. You must accomplish two things: find customers who will pay you fairly for your services, and control your business spending to enable you to make a profit. Many small businesses, especially new ones, find that their cash flow is out of control and, even though accounts-receivable are healthy, they do not have the money on hand to pay bills or payroll on time. This is where budgeting and cost controls become critical.

Your company's cost controls begin with the first item you pay for, whether it is a shovel, a truck, or an accountant. It is to your advantage to shop around, determine the going rate for your target purchase, and look for discounts on that rate. A small accounting firm that specializes in small businesses may offer lower rates than a large firm that demands higher rates to cover the overhead costs of a fancier office and numerous employees. You may also find the service is more personal when dealing with a small law firm or accounting practice.

Know your costs

Never blindly accept any price. Ask yourself how any product or service can be obtained for less money. You may not get as low of a price as a chain store or big business, but you do have the ability to move to lower cost suppliers who will deliver the quality you expect. As you put together your monthly, quarterly, and annual budgets and cost estimates, plan to spend as little as possible. When you start out in business, it is wise to stick to the basics and save the luxuries for a later day. It may be tempting to be a bit extravagant here and there: a nice leather chair for your office, a fancier desk, a warehouse for your equipment, but you cannot make money if you are spending it all. Develop a frugal mind-set. Use this form to identify some of your expenses, then see what you may be able to reduce and by how much:

Know your costs

Utilities:

Gas	$_____
Electricity	$_____
Water	$_____
Sewage	$_____

Office:

Supplies	$_____
Equipment leases	$_____
Postage	$_____

Insurance:

Vehicle	$_____
Workers' Compensation	$_____
General liability	$_____
Health	$_____
Life/Key Man	$_____

Loans

Business	$_____
Vehicle	$_____
Equipment	$_____

Marketing:

Yellow pages	$_____
Mailings	$_____
Printed material	$_____
Cost of sales	$_____
Other	$_____

Dues:

Chamber of Commerce	$_____
Professional organization	$_____
Business Network Intl	$_____
Other	$_____

Equipment Maintenance

Vehicle	$_____
Mower(s)	$_____
Blower(s)	$_____
Other	$_____

Employee(s)

Full-time	$_____
Part-time	$_____

Cost of business

Fuel	$_____
Oil	$_____
Parts	$_____
Uniforms	$_____
Safety	$_____

Special expenses

Subcontractors (per job)	$_____
Materials	$_____
One-time costs	$_____

This list may grow much longer. As you go about your day-to-day business operations, you will no doubt come across other items to add. Note and categorize every dollar you spend, then to find ways to either eliminate the expense or get it cheaper.

Utilities

With utility deregulation underway in some states, you may be able to negotiate your gas or electric rate by considering alternate suppliers. In the past, a business had to be very large or use vast amounts of energy to bargain for better rates. That is not always true today — some states even offer alternate energy suppliers for residential customers.

There are also numerous ways to reduce your consumption of gas and electricity. It may seem inconsequential to save pennies on your electricity bill, but if you start there and force similar savings on everything you do, in the long run the pennies will add up.

Low-energy light bulbs are good for the environment and use less electricity. There are many brands and options. Take advantage of them. If you have gas heat, make sure the system is working efficiently and has a clean filter. If you are working out of your home and are taking a tax deduction for your office space, be aware that basic cost efficiencies in your home will eventually translate into dollars for you. Take your utility company's advice and perform an energy audit of your home and office.

Water should not be a major expense at your office or your home, unless you maintain a significant plant inventory and therefore must use copious amounts of water to keep them healthy. If that is the case, look into ways to conserve or recycle water, such as cisterns to capture rainwater.

Office Expenses

The office is a good place to control costs. If you can develop systems and strategies that keep your operating costs down, even a few cents at a time, it will add up in the long run.

Let us take stationery, for example. As a landscaper, nursery owner, or yard maintenance firm, your business does not need the same fancy linen stationery that would be appropriate for a major law firm. Basic paper stock is fine. A professional-looking letterhead with a single color will suffice. That may change if you begin working in high-end neighborhoods where your customers prefer that the services they purchase are top-of-the-line, but right now conserving upfront expenditures is the best strategy. Envelopes, business cards, order forms, contracts, and other forms can look crisp and professional at low cost. Some forms you can print yourself. You may buy office supplies online through a discount supplier, or buy from an office supply warehouse. Buy in bulk if you will use a lot of the product, but avoid oversupply (especially if you have limited storage in your office.

If you lease equipment for such services as credit card processing and postage, shop around for the best deal. Practice your negotiating skills on everything, and with all vendors, whether or not your target product or service is advertised on sale. You may be shocked by the price variations for the same service with the same piece of equipment. Keep in mind that every vendor you deal with has the same goals you have for your business: gaining the highest possible margins. Beware of unnecessary upgrades a company may try to sell, and keep your basic goal of quality in mind while covering the essentials.

Loans

If you borrowed money to go into business, or arranged for a line of credit to purchase equipment or smooth your cash flow, you must budget to make repayments. Seek out the lowest interest rates and the best terms for the money. Fees, closing costs, document processing can raise the cost of borrowing money, so apply the same standards here as you would apply to vendors. If your credit is good, you will discover that most lenders are happy to deal with you and are willing to negotiate. If your credit is not so good, it may mean higher interest rates, increased fees, and special charges. Do your best to improve your credit score by borrowing as little as possible, paying on time and in full. Eventually, if you maintain good financial habits, your credit score will rise and the cost of borrowing money will go down.

Marketing

Marketing is essential to your business's well being, but it can also be a budget-buster. We will discuss marketing in detail in Chapter 13, but your annual marketing plan is likely to include the telephone book's yellow pages and similar publications. Avoid the temptation to go for a full-page advertisement, despite what a salesperson may tell you about its benefits. You will want a yellow pages presence, but you do not need to spend big dollars. There can be a significant lag-time for such annual ads. If your business is like most start-ups, you will have a limited marketing budget. It is advisable to spread it around to get the best value. The only marketing that is worthwhile *makes you money.*

Dues

Your membership in organizations such as the Chamber of Commerce, Business Networking International (BNI), local or national landscaping and nursery associations, and other professional groups will bring you business, so budget money to pay your dues. Plan to spend several hundred dollars per year for these memberships, plus whatever application or initiation fees are involved. Most of these groups will have some period during the year in which they waive these fees as initiatives to increase membership.

If you find that the cost of membership in all of the groups you identify will not fit in your initial budget, determine which one or two of these organizations will be most beneficial and delay joining the others. Talk to other professionals about the groups they have joined and ask them which provide the most leads or customers. In some cases, BNI produces more residential business than the local Chamber of Commerce, but the Chamber ultimately can offer business-to-business contacts that you might otherwise miss.

There is one unavoidable fact about memberships in business groups: You must show up and be active or you will be wasting your money. Membership alone does not bring in business. You must go to the meetings, pass out your business cards, work a booth at the annual fund-raising picnic, volunteer for whatever charity your group supports, and help other members increase their businesses just as you are asking them to help yours. This requires a commitment of time, which can be in short supply for a small business owner.

Equipment maintenance

This is one area where going cheap is a mistake. Your equipment makes you money, so you must be kind to it. That means following manufacturers' recommendations regarding maintenance and parts replacement. Keep your mowers and other equipment clean, sharp, oiled, and in good working condition. If possible, learn to fix it yourself to save labor costs. Use your downtime to sharpen blades, change oil, inspect spark plugs, and replace cords and other parts. Purchase the highest quality oil at the proper weight and keep a supply in your truck in the event oil levels drop while you are on the job.

Keep a maintenance log and note each repair or replacement of parts and oil. Note the date and frequency of blade sharpening and replacement. Note the cost of maintenance on each piece of equipment. You should be creating a fund to replace equipment when it wears out. When the cost of maintaining any given piece of equipment approaches the cost of replacing it, throw it away and get a new or reconditioned item. Proper maintenance over time will save you money because your equipment will last longer. If you have employees, train them to maintain and repair the equipment they use. If your employee can repair an expensive piece of equipment, this will save you money over time. When an employee performs an otherwise costly repair, give him or her a bonus to show your appreciation. Retention of trained employees is a key way to save money. It saves you from having to find someone else, and spend time and money on training.

Employees

If you choose to hire a full or part-time employee, be aware that the cost can be far higher than you anticipate. Basically, you have two choices to get work done: hire someone who will be employed by your company and whose taxes are deducted by your company, or sign up someone who is an independent contractor — for whom you would file a 1099 income tax form. A person working under a 1099 uses a Federal Tax ID or social security number (if a sole proprietor) and actually operates his/her own business. This type of worker is responsible for his own taxes. Individuals who provide their services to a number of small businesses prefer this arrangement. You may find yourself using this type of worker if all you need is occasional help. You will not be expected to pay benefits or social security deposits for this person, but you must be careful not to refer to independent contractors as "employees," or to demand that they work specified hours, at specified locations, or be under your control. The IRS is aware that businesses may attempt to use contractors to avoid paying payroll taxes. You want to be sure you do not violate the rules for 1099 work. Ask your accountant for an opinion, or check the following IRS sites:

- **www.irs.gov/businesses/small/ article/0,,id=99921,00.html**
  This site will help you determine the difference between employees and independent contractors.

- **www.irs.gov/businesses/small/
  article/0,,id=179115,00.html**
  This site will give you an example of an independent contractor's work and compensation pattern.

An independent contractor is required to choose his or her own times to work. Now, it is possible, even likely, that a potential independent contractor will choose to work the hours you would prefer, but if the contractor wants to take a two-hour lunch break, you are not permitted to punish him or her if the work is done on schedule. If the worker is under your control, he or she is working as an *employee*, not a contractor. Basically, if you utilize an independent contractor, you have the right to control or direct only the *result* of the work, not the means and methods of accomplishing the result.

People who work as independent contractors generally charge more per hour than you would pay an employee because they must pay their entire FICA tax as well as many of their own expenses, marketing costs, and so on. Independent contractors generally work for several different firms, juggling their hours during the week to accommodate several clients. The contractor decides who to work for and when, not the businesses who request his service.

If you use an independent contractor, at tax time you will submit an IRS-approved 1099 form to the contractor, and a separate copy sent directly to the IRS, showing the total compensation that person received from you in the previous year. This is done, in part, to keep the contractor honest. Independent contractors are responsible for reporting all earnings, filing a Schedule C to deduct expenses like any other businesses, and paying all required taxes.

If you hire a full-time employee, expenses for vehicles, insurance, and so on shift to you. In addition to base pay, employers pay the social security tax for each employee (half is the employer's responsibility, the other half is deducted from the employees gross pay), plus Worker's Compensation Insurance, unemployment benefits, and all the other costs associated with maintaining an employee. These additional costs may amount to 24 percent or more over straight base pay. The IRS employer tax information is available in hard copy or online at **www.irs.gov/publications/ p15/ar02.html**

A full-time employee could easily cost your business more than $40,000 per year. You also have to follow labor department guidelines for overtime and other employee-labor rules that are not germane to contractors. One or more full-time employees on your staff means you are writing paychecks every month, even when business is slow. How much business do you need to justify that kind of expense? It is a basic business assumption that employees *make* money for their employers, so you will have to do the math to make this work for you. This involves your level of business and profit margin. You must make enough to pay for employee salaries, and a little more to pay for gas, marketing, insurance, and all of the other costs of doing business before you break even. It is easier to add benefits than to take them away, so be cautious as you go through the hiring process. Your first responsibility is to your business. It is no good for anyone if you are forced to let someone go because you do not have the financial resources to honor your employment package.

If you only need part-time help, you may choose to hire part-time workers for your busy season. Unlike independent contractors, part-time employees are under your control. Although you are required by the government to pay taxes on the amount they earn, just as if they were full-timers, you may not be required to provide certain other benefits that are obligations for full-time help. Check with your accountant and the IRS if you are unsure of your financial responsibilities.

Cost of business

As mentioned above, it takes money just to keep the doors open for business. There will be expenses to be paid whether you have any customers or not. Your truck needs fuel and your power equipment needs oil and spark plugs. You have business cards that need to be replaced because you are passing them out to everyone you meet. There are also the costs of contracts, estimate sheets, and letterhead. Some of your tools will break and be replaced. You will need safety goggles, steel-toed boots, and possibly back braces for heavy lifting.

These and more are the day-to-day expenses of operating a business. Major equipment purchases are one-time expenses and their cost can be spread over time as you work with your accountant to categorize major expenditures, but there is no getting around the need for tight budgeting of the everyday costs you will incur. Examine each category and be tough in your budgeting. Develop driving habits that increase your gasoline mileage. Look for ways to save money and confine your spending to what your business *needs*, not what you *want*.

Products and materials

There is an old saying: "A poor man can afford only the very best." Quality is cheaper in the long run. Just as you are advised to obtain the best tools and equipment you can afford, so must you use the best quality materials available. Whether it is concrete, mulch, or topsoil, stay away from the lowest quality. Bad concrete will crack or fall apart. Questionable topsoil may be full of weeds or be unable to grow much of anything. Even worse, it may contain toxic substances. Before you try to control your costs by cutting back on what you pay for products or materials, be sure you are evaluating only reputable vendors who will make sure that the supplies you purchase from them are as advertised. You do not want to ruin your new business by providing your customers with shoddy or harmful products and materials.

Special expenses

Not every expense can be foreseen. Some items are difficult if not impossible to budget in advance. You can, however, apply your normal tight-fisted budgeting philosophy to special projects or other unusual circumstances.

One such circumstance would be a large project for which you are taking on a subcontractor. In this case, let us assume it is a major landscaping project involving stonework and a small pond. You and your employee can handle most of the work yourselves, but you cannot re-grade or re-contour the yard, so you need to contract with someone to do that. You cannot do the intricate stonework required either, so you need to find someone to do that for you too. You have two requirements for each of these prospective subcontractors: first, are they competent enough to do a good job? Second, is their price fair and can you mark it up and still provide the customer with a project cost that is competitive?

As you budget this project, consider the qualifications of your subcontractors and who will be responsible for cost overruns, project upgrades, and other changes. This is another example of the need for detailed contracts that outline all responsibilities and thorough research of your potential partners in any project. Bear in mind that if you are the primary contractor, the customer will turn to you to resolve problems. If your subcontractors have problems getting the job completed in a satisfactory manner, your customer will turn to you for solutions, not to the subcontractor whose poor grading of the yard created drainage problems that flooded the basement.

Problems will arise. It is a natural part of business. Your contracts should assign responsibility for solving problems and spell out who must pay for what. If you have done your research in your search for subcontractors, you will be more confident that the job will be done right. Re-doing a job can sink a budget and ruin an entire business year.

We will assume that you plan to be in business for a long time and will work hard to develop a reputation as a solid landscaping business. You can only do that by building a list of satisfied customers who are eager to refer you to their friends and colleagues. Angry or disappointed homeowners will drag your business down.

Responsible budget management may mean short-term sacrifices for long-term gain. Avoid the temptation of cutting corners to achieve short-term satisfaction. You are in this for the long run so keep your expenses lean, while acknowledging that every day is an investment in your future and the health of your business.

Setting financial targets

While you are still planning to open your business, you should take the time to lay out an initial budget and do some preliminary income forecasting with your banker and accountant. Set a particular target income the first three years at a minimum. Then, work backwards to figure out how many jobs you will need to reach that income level, and what you will do to find those customers. Taking a hard look at your income potential before you start will place you in a realistic position from the beginning, so you will build and maintain a profitable business.

Evaluating your progress

Even though you have set targets and think you know where the money will be coming from, circumstances change. By reevaluating your business on a monthly or quarterly track to start, then going to an annual evaluation, you will focus on what you are doing, where you are heading, and can make the necessary course corrections. Once again, enlist your accountant in this process. He or she may be able to show you how to compare reports on your software accounting program that will give you the detail you need.

Pricing services

Pricing is the key to your success in the landscaping business. You do not need to be the cheapest in town to land customers. The cheapest lawn service or landscaper may use junk equipment, be unreliable, do shoddy work, and have no license or insurance. Many people assume that the cheapest guy offers the worst product; such people deliberately seek out the midrange or higher-priced vendor, because they believe that a higher price automatically means better quality service. So, being the cheapest game in town may actually cost you customers.

There is nothing automatic about the pricing equation. The rates you set will be justified by the service you deliver and the image you are able to build with your customers. Since you are just starting out, you need to establish some basis for determining the rates you will charge. To begin setting prices, do your homework. Learn what your competitors are charging for the services you provide. Collect information from the same general income level of customers or neighborhood that you plan to serve. You may be able to find out what others charge by phoning them, or recruit a friend or two do this for you. When a competing company sends out an estimator to quote the job, you probably would not want the competitor to come to *your* home to size up the yard.

In addition to asking friends or family members to do some price sleuthing for you, consider asking potential customers. When you pass a homeowner watering the grass of a beautiful yard, stop to ask if he has a lawn service. If the answer is yes, you can say innocently enough, "I bet it is expensive!" At that point, they may offer you the exact amount they pay.

Some business people also find pricing help by asking vendors, industry associations, or by calling landscaping experts in other cities who are not competitors. Keep your eyes and ears open at all times, and whenever there seems to be an opportunity to do a little industry-price investigation, do so. Odds are high that your competitors will not tell you their pricing secrets voluntarily. Think of it as *market research*. Be sure that specific services and products are identified in your pricing research. For instance, you will want all of the quotes friends and family members obtain from competitors to match the services your company provides: lawn mowing, edging, weeding, mulching, and so on.

Examine the quotes you obtain carefully. Look to see if your competitors are adding extra fees for sloping yards, low-hanging tree limbs, animal residue, long driveways, or other special characteristics of the yards. Are their bids broken down into hourly rates or services? Do they provide specific square footage or yard dimensions? What do their bids look like? Are they contracts or simply agreements to provide yard care? Do their bids have conditions?

By learning the policies of companies in your area, you can adapt them to your business affairs. For example, if most other companies have cancellation or change penalties, your customers will likely accept the same conditions from you. Maybe they have bad-weather policies to provide lawn and garden care within a specified amount of time in the event of rain or other weather condition that prevents service on the day of the week listed in the agreement or contract. You want to come across at least as professional and well organized as your competitors, if not more so. By adhering to the norms of your community, or offering something slightly better, you will fit comfortably into the field of competition.

Once you have collected pricing estimates from three or four competitors, you can safely price your services somewhere in the middle, at a profit margin that is fair to you. Always apply your standard overhead cost into the price you quote for your services.

What will you offer?

Take a look at a well-maintained yard and ask yourself what work went into it. The yard had to be graded to drain properly and to be visually appealing. A certain type of grass was planted, watered, fed, and mowed to a proper height for climate and other conditions. Trees and shrubs were placed and planted and cared for. Flowerbeds were designed, planted, and maintained. Perhaps there is a patio or deck, maybe even a swimming pool or fountain. Is there a stone wall or a fence? Walkways? Are they brick, stone, or gravel? Check all of the details of this and other yards and gardens you admire and ask yourself what aspects of this overall look you are capable of performing. Can you already provide this level of gardening and, perhaps, reach an even higher level?

Unless you have training, experience, and a contractor's license, you might want to stay away from designing and grading yards. Bulldozing, installing or correcting drainage systems, land contouring, and berm construction (adding mounds of earth) may require special licensing and certainly demands a level of experience and skill that cannot be obtained entirely from book learning. Taking a job as an apprentice for an experienced landscape contractor may set you on the right path for this type of work.

However, you may already feel comfortable designing flowerbeds or placing trees and bushes to create a pleasing effect. Again, if you do not have any training in this area, it might be a service you can put off until you obtain the proper credentials. Many community colleges offer landscape design courses, some for certification. Such programs are worth exploring for those in the landscape and garden industry.

The basic services most new outdoor service businesses will offer are lawn care, maintenance, and mulching. Tasks will include mowing, edging, and weeding. Most landscape companies include edging as part of the mowing price; weeding and mulching are separate services and are separately priced. Many beginners in this field offer these basic services while they build their customer base and become more comfortable with the industry and their place within it. As time passes and your customer base builds, you can begin to offer more sophisticated and expensive services such as design and construction of landscape elements. It is typical in the growth of an outdoor service business that the owner starts out with yard maintenance and moves into more challenging and lucrative landscaping over time. While it is nice to have a few $50 lawn customers, it is even nicer to have a few $5,000 landscape jobs, or even $50,000 projects that include substantial design and construction.

The key points are that you should offer the services you are comfortable doing, once you are confident that you can do them well, on time, and make a profit on your work.

You must control costs and be aware of every penny that comes in and goes out. Bidding on a $50,000 job that will cost you $51,000 is not a good business move, even though it looks good on paper from a gross volume point of view. Do not be fooled by the notion that sometimes it is good to lose a little money if you are gaining experience. You cannot take experience to the bank to pay your bills. Get your credentials through training, not through bad business management.

Chapter Eight

Estimates, Bids, and Contracts

Contracts with Vendors

Vendors provide the supplies and services that keep your business running smoothly. Just as with every aspect of business, building solid relationships with suppliers is the path to long-term business success and profitability. If you earn your vendors' trust over time, they may be willing to cut you some slack during those hopefully rare times when your bank account is squeezed. On the other hand, you do not want to rely too heavily on the good will of your vendors, especially early in your relationship, or overpromise your potential value as a customer to them. Mutual respect between vendor and yourself as customer is the goal.

What types of vendors will your business need to function? There are the general services that most businesses work with, such as the local media or ad agencies that run your advertising programs if you create and buy advertising; the printer who prints your flyers, if you do not print them yourself; your phone service, your Internet service provider and Web site developer, and your health insurance provider.

As a landscaping or lawn care service, you will rely on vendors from whom you buy fertilizers, lawn seed, lawn mowing and edging equipment, garden tools, and nurseries or plant and tree wholesalers. Some of these vendors may offer you special commercial contracts, viewing you as a fellow professional in the business. There are many advantages to arranging a commercial account, including discounts in some cases, but you may have to negotiate this with someone beyond the sales clerk level to get your business plugged into the system. Usually, you have to supply banking and credit references, which are sometimes difficult to obtain when you are just starting out.

If you have good credit, you may be able to establish a line of credit with important vendors, allowing you to charge the goods or materials you need for your customers and pay in thirty days. This is a distinct advantage for you, because the supplier carries your upfront cost while you take care of your customer. Then you get paid, and subsequently pay the vendor.

A purchase order is a contract you make with a vendor that specifies exactly what and to whom the material is to be given. There are several advantages in utilizing purchase orders. By officially giving notice to your vendors that you will always supply a purchase order for any charge, you will avoid mistakes that might permit an unauthorized person to wrongly bill a purchase to your account. Purchase orders also provide complete records of transactions with individual vendors, so you can easily track how much of a particular product you buy. Because purchase order numbers are noted on vendor invoicing, all cost changes will easily monitored too. Even if your credit history does not give you the option to set up commercial accounts immediately when you open, you can still start your business. You should simply expect to "pay retail" until you can demonstrate to your vendors that you are seriously engaged in business and will be a profitable customer for them.

Another way many small business startups buy supplies is to use national credit cards, such as MasterCard, Visa, or Discover. Credit card interest rates are usually higher than individual vendor credit lines, and the opportunity to build a close vendor/customer relationship is less compelling, but credit cards may give you the chance to make partial payments, not pay the entire bill in thirty days. Just be sure you pay the credit card company on time. Late fees involve serious penalties that will destroy your profitability in a hurry, while simultaneously damaging your credit rating and business reputation among vendors.

Contracts for Customers

Customer contracts require a different type of approach than contracting with vendors. There are several different ways to present your rates to your potential customer, including estimates and bids, which accomplish different things. A *bid* is a commitment to honor a particular price given particular circumstances, but an *estimate* is your best guess as to what the charge will be, but is not legally binding. With an estimate you imply "I am not exactly sure what this will cost." This approach is most effective when details are sketchy or you prefer to give a price range rather than a firm price. A landscaping assignment may present many hidden challenges; you may not know in advance where problems lurk. For example, a stone in a yard may look small on the surface, but if you agree to remove it for a set price, then later find out it is a huge boulder that is mostly hidden underground and that it requires a bulldozer to move it, you are in trouble. By telling your customer that the rock-removal fee you present is an *estimate*, you alert him or her to the fact that the price is subject to change if unpredictable conditions cause the labor or materials charge to rise.

You will also want to provide an estimate if your potential customer seems unsure of exactly what he or she wants to have done, or is simply "price shopping." If you like, give an hourly rate and include phrases like "a typical fee might be . . ." to retain the necessary wiggle room that allows you to adjust charges if circumstances warrant.

A *bid*, on the other hand, is a promise to perform a task at a specific price. Bids are legally binding. You must fulfill the task as promised, at the stated price, or risk being sued. Large commercial or government jobs ordinarily require a competitive bid. You can expect to have many competitors if the work you bid on is desirable, so make your bid as detailed and specific as possible. There should be no questions about what you promised to do, or what the customer promised to pay for. Bids for projects involving a government entity are public; your pricing detail will be seen by anyone who chooses to examine it. If a vaguely specified bid is accepted at all, it may be subject to questions or arguments by the customer ("But you agreed to do so-and-so.") Some customers decide not to pay if the job was not performed to their expectations. If you have a contract, you can sue to collect, but lawsuits cost everyone time, money, and energy. Better to take the time up front and submit an accurate, detailed bid that both you and the customer understand thoroughly. A clear agreement can help prevent lawsuits.

Contractual details

You have talked to your customer about what he or she wants from you, the landscaping professional. It may be a simple mowing agreement or something more complicated, involving flower beds and walkways. You have made notes of everything the customer said to you about the job and his or her expectations. You have drawings of the yard and what your plan for it is. It is time for the signed agreement, or contract. There is no one-size-fits-all contract for landscape and gardening agreements. Requirements vary by state. This is another area where you should consult with an attorney or call state advisors to ensure you are complying with state laws regarding such contracts. Each state has its own requirements on terms of cancellation, environmental regulations, conflict resolution, and so on. Failure to comply can cost you money down the line. For instance, if you choose to be an old-fashioned person who seals deals with a handshake and a smile, be aware that handshake is worthless if your customer decides he or she does not like the work you have done, or feels you have not fulfilled your obligations, and do not have to pay you. You can drag them into small-claims court, but that costs money, time, and no guarantee that you will win the case.

The state of Maryland, for example, is one of many states that allow homeowners three working days to cancel orders or contracts signed in their homes. You, as the provider of goods and services, are required to notify the customer in writing of that right. The wording of that notification is specified in state law and must be included on contracts to be signed by customers. Failure to fulfill these requirements allows the customer to cancel the contract at any time and get his money back. If the customer can prove that you did not inform him of the right to cancel the contract within three business days, he has the right to get back everything he paid to you, no matter what other aspects of the agreement were or were not fulfilled. This is just one example of how your ignorance of the law can set you up for a potential catastrophe. You have an obligation to yourself and your business to learn and comply with all of your state's contract requirements.

State-approved, pre-printed contracts may be available on the Internet or in your local office supply store, but make sure they are current. State laws change, and the regulatory agency in your state will not give you a break simply because you purchased and used outdated contract forms. It is your responsibility to comply. Your lawyer or the local Chamber of Commerce, State Department of Development, or Attorney General's office will be able to guide you to the appropriate contracting terms and procedures.

When a job is quoted, be certain you put *everything* in the contract. If you are going to mow the grass, state the size of the lawn. If it includes edging, put it in the contract. Specify weeding, clipping, and mulching as desired in the contract. If the customer will pay weekly, state the terms. If this is a monthly or seasonal contract, specify the details and payment schedule. The point is to avoid misunderstandings. Customers always have a right to cancel a contract for nonperformance or, in most cases, general dissatisfaction. Consult your attorney about your state's laws concerning cancellation of these types of contracts and the rights of each side. However, you want to avoid producing large contracts with fine print, especially with residential customers. Potentially good customers could become offended or wary, wondering why you need all the formalities. Simply be specific, meet legal requirements on your contracts, and do a good landscaping job. That will keep you in business.

Planning for Profitability

Have you already figured out how much you have to earn per hour to "succeed" on your own terms? If not, start with this simple example. As previously mentioned, begin with the amount of money you need to bring into your business every month just to pay your bills. If you assume that number is, say, $5,000, that means that every day you need to bring in at least $167. Many businesses do not operate every day of the month, so let us assume you will work six days a week, at least in your first few months in business. That gives you four weeks at six days per week, for a total of 24 working days during the month. Now your daily earning requirement is $208, or $26 per hour for an eight-hour workday, just to meet your expenses on our hypothetical $5,000 per month cost of doing business. This does not include the marked-up purchase price of products bought by customers through your business. This assumption implies that you are working in the field for eight hours, 24 days per month. Time in your office or on sales calls is not directly compensated, although you should factor this average time into the overhead percentage you include in pricing a job.

Looking at these numbers, the break-even minimum you can charge is $52 for two hours of work. At that rate, you would not be making any profit at all. You would be working for free. So, even with the goal of "building business," you cannot charge $30 for two hours of work. If a customer expects this rate, you have to say no. You would have trouble making a reasonable income at $30 for one hour. New businesses are tempted to throw out low numbers to get customers, but it will catch up to you. There also is a temptation to throw in free services to help close a deal, but these too will bring down your financial position. Consider the case of a hypothetical customer who likes to bargain for lower prices on most of what she buys. This type of person may sense that you are new and vulnerable, so she makes it clear that the most she will pay is $20 for the lawn care that will take you a half hour for each mowing, and she wants free weeding in spring and fall and free mulching of the flowerbed. Your mowing rate alone would come to $40 per hour at this rate, which does not sound too bad at first. But, in six months your total work for this customer will include four mows a month for six months at the demanded $20 per mow. That comes to $480 over the season from this customer. However, you have to figure in another six to eight hours for the free spring and fall weeding, which takes a lot of time, plus the cost of buying and spreading the mulch.

Even using conservative time estimates, you could easily be giving away seven hours of work or $280 of your time, not counting the purchase of the mulch you would spread. This would bring down your "income" from this customer to $200 for the season. Your actual earnings would plummet to $17 per hour, not $40, just by tossing in the so-called "free" services and mulch. You would not only face zero profitability, you would not break even. Walk away.

If you use the methods previously described to test the competitive rates in your community, and if you price your work accordingly, many if not most of your customers will be quite happy with your price. All you must do to keep their business is what you promised. It is usually better to find those customers who are willing to pay you a fair price. Too often, customers who pay the least demand the most. Said customer would not only want free weeding and mulch, but might also complain about how badly it was done, which would require you to do it again. If you track your costs and time carefully, you will soon learn to charge a price that is fair to you and your customer for every service and product you provide. You do not want to be in a position where you must do so many jobs to stay afloat that your service slips because you are racing from one place to the next.

Bidding for Commercial Jobs

Commercial jobs can be good, steady work, but likely will not provide you with the high profit margins you can and should get from small residential customers. There are many reasons for this but the primary is the size of the jobs. Builders, property managers, and homeowners associations are all potential commercial contract sources.

Builders and developers need landscape design and maintenance services for their projects and are always looking for reliable companies. New companies make the mistake of taking on more work than they can handle. As the owner you want to grow your business, so when a property manager says he has a $10,000-per-month contract up for bids you may be excited about the prospect of the high pay, But can you handle the job?

Remember our successful landscape company owner who told us, "Landscaping doesn't lend itself to increased profitability with increased size." Profitability is the key. When you bid on a commercial job be sure you can actually do it. Let us take a look at the $10,000-per-month contract that is up for bids.

What is involved here? Will you be mowing, edging, and trimming, or installing watering systems, repairing and replacing sidewalks? Will you need a backhoe or bulldozer? How many employees will you need, and how much will they cost? What type of insurance will you need and how much will it cost? Do you have the necessary permits and licenses for this type of work? Will you need subcontractors? Is it better for you to *be* a subcontractor on this? Can you actually do this work? Can you make any money? What are the terms of the contract and how will you be paid?

The first question you must answer, of course, is whether you can do the work required. Be realistic. If you are new to this business, you may want to pass on ambitious projects until you have a better grasp of what it takes to fulfill them. Look at the scope of work to be done, determine the number of hours required to do it, the material and equipment you will need, factor in bad weather and unforeseen problems, add up your costs, and a profit margin you can live with. Is it doable? What are your upfront costs? What do you have to buy or rent?

Let us assume now that you have decided to go for it. You have looked at the numbers and the scope of work and plan to move forward and bid on this job. Commercial managers do not normally engage in a lot of negotiation with their contractors. "Here is what we want, this is what we are willing to pay," is a typical standard. Your bid will be measured against others and it is likely that the decision will be made on the property manager's opinion of your ability to get the job done.

If you win the bid, you must get to work and get paid. How will you be paid? You are facing considerable upfront costs in terms of equipment, insurance, and employees who want to be paid in a timely manner. Is there any upfront money in the contract? How will you survive if the contract does not pay you for 30 or even 60 days after the start of work? Do you have the cash reserves or a credit line to fill the financial gap?

If you chose to bid on commercial projects it is best to start small and work up. An ideal contract would be with a homeowners association where you would be only required to maintain a common area of a residential development, cutting grass, weeding, and planting flowers. It is manageable and allows you to show off your services to every homeowner entering and leaving the development. These types of contract provide steady income and help pay the bills, allowing you to take on an employee or two, which allows you to take on more work. That way you can build slowly toward the bigger commercial contracts without facing cash issues.

As you build toward this goal you also are adding value to your business. Instead of being burdened with heavy debt, you are in a financially healthy position. The first goal, of course, is to get out there and network to meet the people who will be in a position to use your company to maintain commercial landscaping properties as you build your business.

Always keep in mind that you may need to continually refine your pricing strategy, based on your direct experience with customers in your market. Your intent is to have your customer feel the price is reasonable, while you are assured of a profit. If you bid too high, the homeowner will not hire you. If you bid too low, you will not make enough money to pay yourself, or possibly to cover your direct costs. Your business will go under in a short time. So your basic pricing strategy will always be aimed to strike the happy medium. If the customer with whom you are negotiating is unwilling to pay what is necessary to make a profit, walk away. Chances are you will be losing a problem, not an asset. You will simultaneously demonstrate that you expect proper compensation for the high level of your services.

Negotiating Prices

"Can you bring your price down?"

This is a question new business owners face frequently, so be prepared for it. If you have priced the job fairly, which means you have included a reasonable profit for yourself, and the customer will be receiving high-quality services and products, the answer is "no."

Say you are talking to a potential customer about a range of services such as lawn maintenance, installation of a flower garden, and trimming bushes and trees over the course of the season. It is a 10,000-square-foot yard and has a rather severe slope on one side. Your price is $60 per week for the lawn care, including edging, plus $1,500 for the installation of the flowerbed and another $1,500 for the bushes and trees. You are in an area with an eight-month season. The lawn maintenance totals $1,920 and the two other services come to $3,000, for a total of $4,920. The customer tells you he or she budgeted $4,000 for all of it and asks you to bring your price down.

When you hear the question, take it seriously. Try not to scoff or look startled. Your first step should be to take a deep breath and smile. It may take practice but you can learn to say no with a smile, when someone starts to dismantle your bid into small components to chip away at the prices. If you price fairly at the outset, it will not be hard to explain that you cannot afford to cut ten percent off the top, just because the total job is larger than most. You can sympathize with your client and say that you understand he or she would like to pay less. Then ask which service(s) he or she would like to modify or eliminate, rather than countering with a lower price. If you immediately offer to cut your price, you undermine your credibility and risk losing your profit.

By asking, "What would you like to eliminate?" your customer is now responsible for determining the outcome – not you. Your price per service is fair and you should hold to it. If your client has budgeted $4,000 for what fairly costs $4,920, it is his or her option to pay the fair price or modify the scope of work. While it is possible that he or she will decide to look for someone cheaper, this is not a bad outcome. If the $920 price difference represents your profit on this job, you are better off moving on to the next customer than working for free.

Most people understand the concept of a fair price for a quality service and product. Work with your customers to help them achieve their landscaping goals by offering plans that meet their budgets. Perhaps this customer can wait for her flowerbed. You could even suggest what a great project that might be for next year. Keep smiling, and be professional and friendly. Remember, you are trying to establish mutually comfortable, long-term relationships.

Billing and Collection

The first rule of billing is: do it promptly. Especially when you are just getting started, cash flow is likely to be a problem. With small landscaping jobs, payment upon completion is appropriate. You want to invoice your customers as soon as the work is finished. Present the bill in person, the day you finish the yard, if you can. If you are able to hand the bill to your customer, it is impossible for that person to say that it must have been lost in the mail.

Once you are busy it is more efficient to prepare and mail a group of bills together, on a regular schedule, such as twice a month, on the 15th and the 30th. Yard maintenance contracts are typically billed monthly. Extensive landscaping contracts, such as a complete landscaping design and installation, may be divided into multiple payments over time. It is up to you whether you would prefer to "hold" these accounts, billing and receiving payment directly, or whether you would rather arrange with a bank to have credit card processing so your customers can "charge it." The advantage of accepting credit card payments is your payment will arrive in one installment. The disadvantage is the fee that will come off the top of your payment, or as a monthly charge, which can be substantial, depending on your volume.

Most word processing software packages have templates for statements that you can tailor to your business if you do not want to pay for customized forms from an agency. All you really need to prepare a statement is a letterhead that includes your business name, address, and contact information such as a Web site, e-mail address, and phone or fax numbers. Type in the customer's name, address, and the date and fill in the details of what the customer is paying for, and the amount owed.

Finally, do not forget to write in the payment terms, such as "thirty days net" or "Payment due upon receipt." Some business owners offer a discount for prompt payment as an option to speed receipt of funds.

If you operate a nursery, especially if you are planning to sell plants wholesale, you may find that you will need to offer favorable credit terms to your customers as well as receiving credit from vendors. The easiest solution, as mentioned earlier, is to set up credit card processing. If you decide to extend the credit yourself to save credit card fees, make sure to check the credit history of your client. Do not just request credit references — get on the telephone and verify them. Extending credit to small, undercapitalized landscaping firms may put your own fledgling business at risk. You should also add on an interest charge for late payments. You are operating a landscape or nursery business, not a bank.

In addition, be sure that you do not fill purchase orders based only on the purchase order number. Insist on a mailed or faxed hardcopy of the purchase order itself. A customer's employee could use a purchase order number without authorization by the person in charge. If the boss balks at paying for this order, and you have only the number, not a sheet of paper with the order specified and signed by the customer, you may have a hard time collecting. If, however, you have the detailed purchase order, it is a binding contract and the customer legally must pay, regardless of who made the request.

When landscaping or nursery businesses undertake large jobs or orders, especially if products or plants are purchased, it is justifiable to demand that customers prepay 10 to 50 percent. This gives you some assurance that the customer is committed to the plan you have negotiated. Such foresight will protect you from having products you cannot use if the customer changes his or her mind.

Secrets of Job Estimating

Learning how to estimate a job and price it right for both your business and your community is the secret to a successful business. Ideally, you will get it right from day one. More realistically—you will make some mistakes, and "eat" some jobs, on the way to getting experience in your new venture. Do not be too hard on yourself if you occasionally under price or overprice your services at the beginning. (You will know you have overpriced a service if the customers regularly go elsewhere.) Keep track of what you estimate for which services, and to whom. Also note when you succeed in selling the job, and when you fail. Go over these records every week or two, at first. Once you have gained experience you may be able to let the records wait and review them once a month. To operate successfully, you need to stay aware of what you are doing, what works, what does not work, and what you might want to try differently. Regular evaluation will help you achieve this important analysis.

Create task breakdowns

It goes without saying that not every task in lawn care should be billed the same. Even if your customer winds up seeing a single hourly rate or project rate on the invoice, you—the owner of the company — need to track what it really costs to do part x, y, or z of any particular job. One helpful way to track these costs is to do a task breakdown on each project. You may not need to go into such detail forever, but during your business start-up period, it is a very good idea.

What is a "task breakdown"? It is an itemized list of all the different parts of the job that will be performed for a given customer. It starts with the most basic task of all — getting to and from the job site. Put "transportation" at the top your list. Make a separate column for miles and/or time it takes to get to the job site, and from the job site to the next job. Add in the estimated cost of gasoline, and a factor to cover overhead on your truck. Even if the overhead is just $1, it is useful to see it on paper, for every trip you take and every job you do.

Other tasks will vary according to the work you perform. Tasks may include such items as mowing, edging, mulching, trimming, weeding, pruning, planting, raking, and more. You should also put in a separate category for cleanup. If you are designing a landscape, or digging a fresh garden space, those are separate tasks. For each category, if there is a logical overhead cost, such as mower maintenance, make a column and put down your best guess. Do not omit string for the string trimmers, oil for the chain saw, and so on. This sort of detail at the start will help you plan for the future, and soon you will automatically see the constellation of expenses that are generated by every use of a particular piece of equipment.

If you are using an extra employee or contractor on a particular job, include the cost of these additional people on the task breakdown as well. The goal of your record is to compile a comprehensive view of what is involved on a particular job. It will also help you to see where you may be able to cut costs, or when you need to get outside assistance to perform a particular task. At the end of the task breakdown, leave space to write in what you actually bid for this job, whether the customer accepted the bid, and when you were paid. Save all of the task breakdowns for the first few months of your business. They will be a valuable reference source for evaluating what you are doing right in your business management, and what areas may need correction or rethinking.

Bids you can live with

If you have always worked for someone else, it may be challenging for you to calculate how to set the fees you will be charging so you can support yourself, your family, and your business. You can figure rates in a variety of ways – per square foot, per hour, or per project. It is important to be realistic about what you need to survive, and what you can actually get from your existing market. Let us consider the hourly rate approach, to start. This will give you a realistic target to weigh projects and to evaluate your charge per square foot, should you choose to use those methods in actual practice.

To determine the income-target you require, remember that as an independent businessperson you must pay all your overhead, health benefits, vacation pay, retirement savings and taxes. Total cost of living for you and your family, plus all business expenses and overhead should be added together. Then divide this figure by billable hours to figure the minimum per hour you need to stay afloat. If you work a 50 hour workweek, for 50 weeks (giving yourself some vacation time) that gives you a total of 2,500 work hours, on average, per year. (Working 40 hours per week will give you just 2,000 hours total.)

However, you will not be able to charge directly for all of those hours. You cannot run your business without setting aside regular time for marketing, maintaining equipment, and other non-billable work. Billable hour estimates range from 1,500 to 2,000 hours per year, if you are working 50 hours each week. A quick estimate takes hourly rate x 2000 hours to project your potential annual income: i.e., $40 hour x 2,000 hours = annual income of $80,000...which has to cover all those expenses you previously identified. If you want to make a profit, you will have to earn more than that amount. Also, to fulfill this goal, you will need 2,000 hours of billable work.

Use your estimated hourly rate to help you prepare project rates—a single all-inclusive fee for yard maintenance (for example) by the month or season. Many customers prefer monthly or seasonal contracts, since they know the total cost in advance. The benefit to you is having some degree of predictability in income.

Evaluating the Competition

The outdoor services business is a highly competitive industry because a lawn care business can be started at relatively low cost. How can you keep up with the constant flux of information detailing who is doing what, where they are doing it, how well they do it, and what they charge?

Attending local professional group events will help this process. Whether visiting your area Chamber of Commerce, or the local chapter of the American Nursery and Landscape Association, the conversation of your associates and peers will likely bring tid-bits of information that you can piece together into a better understanding of the competitive atmosphere that surrounds you. You can invite responses from former customers, or suppliers, by simply asking for information. When you see a particularly well-done yard, stop and ask who does the work. On the other hand, if you see a yard disaster in the making, you may want to pay close attention to avoid duplicating the mistake.

One rule that most business people accept is to not speak nega-tively about your competitor in public. If you bad-mouth a com-petitor, often the customer will feel less comfortable with you — even if you are many times more experienced and qualified than the person you are putting down. Staying polite and profession-al — by emphasizing what you do best, and basically ignoring what the competition does — is not only socially acceptable, it is likely to bring you more business.

It is vital to create a formula that includes overhead and profit requirement for your business before beginning to quote pric-es to potential customers. It may not be a good idea to find out what your competition charges and duplicate that rate without checking to see if it works for you. Perhaps your competition is losing money. Competitors have different cost structures. Your bids should be shaped on the cost structure of *your* business — your overhead, your employees, your profit goals — not on Tom's Lawn Service down the street. While it is important to know what your competitors charge for the services you plan to offer or are already providing, your basic pricing method, whether it is by square foot, rate per hour, or a complex, detailed bidding process, has to be localized to be effective.

National average prices for services are of limited use to a business start-up, although a look at trends for the past several years may be helpful to see whether the work is likely to increase. For a general guideline, national average prices are updated annually in various publications, such as *Lawn and Landscape* magazine's annual *State of the Industry Report* that is published in the fall. These surveys will have helpful information about the landscape and garden business suitable for long-range tracking. The U.S. Department of Labor also tracks information about a number of workforce and industry segments in its *Occupational Outlook Report* on the Department of Labor Website at **www.dol.gov**.

Price Strategy and Preparing Bids

Successful outdoor service companies tailor their pricing to suit their community. Most communities will not fit the national average numbers precisely. The salaries and costs where you work may vary by substantial amounts, above or below average. You can always double-check your competitors' prices by doing a little price sleuthing.

You will find out quickly if your fees are within the normal range for your area by the responses customers give you when they receive your bids. If every bid is accepted without hesitation, you may be charging too little. If you are being turned down regularly, ask why. If the answer is usually "too expensive" then either you are contacting the wrong customers for your business plan, or you have priced yourself out of the market.

However, let us get past a great myth: You do not need to be the cheapest lawn and garden service in town to do well. "We're known as being expensive and good and very responsive," is how one successful landscaping company owner puts it. Being known as expensive is not necessarily bad. Note how he added "good and very responsive." That is what his customers are paying for: quality service and customer care. This man, and others like him, are not out to be the cheapest, nor do they think cheap is good. He targets upper-income neighborhoods and offers homeowners quality, not discounts. Although he does have to address price issues now and then, he is not afraid to walk away from a job that will not produce a sufficient profit. He is not in business to provide charity lawn mowing. If you plan to run a successful business, your goal must be to keep your company profitable. Once you are running smoothly, and making the money you require, you can donate your time and energy to those less fortunate. Until then, you must screen out customers who cannot afford your fees.

When you are preparing to quote a job, interview the customer, and take a good look at the yard in question. Never give a top-of-the-head estimate on cost without seeing the yard itself. Preparing estimates that are fair to the customer and your business is perhaps the most challenging aspect of running a lawn care or landscaping business. Many long-experienced lawn specialists guess how long it will take them to maintain a particular yard, but it is essential to visit the lawn personally. If you bid without viewing the property, you take a huge risk that this plot of ground has not had maintenance for the last few years. It could take three times as long as the "average" property of its size. Giving an estimate based on the square-footage alone can sink any potential profit out of sight.

As you determine the scope of work, check the condition of the area where you will be working. If the customer has been using another company, find out which company has had the business and why they are losing it. Also, if possible, find out how much the customer has been paying. One landscaping/gardening company owner recalls a homeowner whose yard looked great but who wanted another company to take over. It turned out that the homeowner was just looking for someone cheaper. The company that already had the business was already giving the guy a great price. There would be no profit for the new company to try to underbid, so that owner told the residential customer he could not beat the price of his current lawn service company, and walked away from the "opportunity."

While conducting your yard evaluation, look for all factors that might interfere with your proposed work or other conditions that contribute to the overall appearance of the area you will be servicing. If the surface of the yard is rough or bumpy, if it is pocked by mole or gopher hills or has noticeable drainage, rock, or other problems, be prepared to address them. Do not promise a beautiful yard if all you will be doing is mowing something that needs a lot more than a mower. Even wealthy people look for bargains. Price is likely to be a consideration in your bid, but make sure you can actually turn a profit on any job you bid on.

Your people-skills are critical to succeed in this business. Look and listen, then repeat back to the customer what you hear to make sure you grasp the nature of what he or she wants. Pay attention to what the customer tells you, and read between the lines. If you are alert, you will probably sense whether this person will be easy or difficult to work with by the way he or she talks about previous projects or companies. Find out how long the customer has lived in this location and how he or she happened to come by the property. This is more than "small talk." You will be finding out what kind of commitment the homeowner has to the property, how important it is to him, whether the yard and garden's appearance is related to his sense of pride. For future up selling, you will benefit by knowing what he wants in the short run and over the next couple of years. Ask what it will take to meet this person's expectations, likes and dislikes. Write it all down, as completely as possible. Be certain you make note of any promises you give the customer.

Then politely ask for time to prepare your pricing for the job, one or two days. Also ask whether or not the homeowner wants a seasonal rate or a one-month trial. (Charge more for a single month, then discount that monthly price if the customer chooses a full season contract in advance.) Factor all of the knowledge you have gained in your yard evaluation and customer interview into your bid or price. Type it up neatly, or print it on a form legibly. Then print out a clear, clean copy to present to your customer, and keep an identical copy for yourself.

Do not forget that there is a major difference between an estimate and a quote or bid. An *estimate* is what you think the cost to the customer will be, based on your best guess given the facts at hand. The *quote* or *bid* is a commitment to do a particular type of work or set of tasks, with or without purchased products, for a specified amount of money. You always can change your figures if the customer changes his or her specifications or if the yard measurements are your customer gave you are clearly incorrect, but a bid must be honored within its specifications. Be sure of your numbers and your commitment for the work before you give the customer a locked-in contract price.

As you plan this job look for ways to up sell the job in the future. The customer may be looking only for lawn care at that moment, but there could be opportunities to provide more services later. For instance, if the yard has flowerbeds or areas that could be prepared as flowerbeds, make a note and offer to provide plans and plantings in the spring. You are the professional and you will see opportunities to improve the appearance of the yard or garden. Your creative ideas are offered to help your customer. If you do a good job in the beginning of your professional relationship, the customer will be more receptive to your ideas about additional services. Your goal is to establish a business consisting of many congenial relationships that last for years. As you encounter your customer time and again, you will have more opportunities to offer fertilizing, aeration, and construction of walkways, patios, fences or trellises. If your relationship works out, and customer satisfaction is achieved, you are likely to expand that basic cut-the-grass homeowner into a year-round garden and yard maintenance customer who pays more to get more.

Pricing guidelines

To base your pricing on what your competitors are charging for the same services you offer, let us hypothetically consider a 10,000-square-foot lawn. You have a new 54-inch mower. The wide mower will allow you to cut the grass faster than the high school kid who is using a 21-inch model which will require him to spend more time going back-and-forth across the yard to get the grass cut. If he is charging $50, you can beat that price because you will be finished and loaded while he will still be sweating and pushing.

However, there is a good chance that high school kids will not be your only competitors. Your new business may be up against professionals who have experience and good equipment too.

Here are a few guidelines that may help you start pricing specific types of jobs:

For lawn mowing only

It never hurts to ask the customer how long it will take to mow their lawn, or ask for the measurements of the lot and figure square footage. Although size of the lot is not the only consideration in pricing, it is a major factor.

If the customer does not know how big the lot is, in acreage, pace it off by walking the length and width of the property. Measure the stride you take, count the number of paces, and multiply the two numbers together to get an estimate of the dimensions. An acre contains 43,560 square feet. If an acre lot is square, it would measure approximately 70 yards by 70 yards, or 208 feet x 208 feet, but many yards are not square. If it is irregular in shape, estimate by multiplying the longest length times the widest width, then reducing the total by eyeballing the area and calculating an approximate percentage. Also subtract spaces that are occupied by outbuildings or other obstacles, such as a shed or garage, flowerbeds, or trees. Each of those objects will need to be trimmed or edged. Be sure to factor in the time required for trimming and edging all the structures, trees, and flowerbeds, as well.

Keep track of the lot sizes you are mowing, and how long it takes you to mow them. Create a chart, listing acreage by fractions (one tenth of an acre to one half acre or more, if you are mowing larger lots.) Then fill in a second column with the time it takes to mow a particular size lot with your equipment. Next time you are asked to mow that particular lot size, you will be able to glance at your chart to give a quicker estimate. Most lawn maintenance experts estimate about 15 minutes to mow a tenth of an acre. If you hire employees, have them keep track of the time they spend per yard as well. The more factual data you have on hand, the easier it is to price your jobs correctly from the beginning. It is much easier to lower a price than to raise it, so be sure you are not cheating yourself on a job by accepting a price that will not cover your costs or give you the profit margin you need.

Some lawn services who focus on residential property stress the profitability of mowing many small lawns per day, rather than two or three large ones. Their rationale is that the mower can earn higher hourly rates with a flat fee for small yards, especially if the yards are in the same neighborhood. Owners of larger properties are more likely to be reluctant to contract for a flat fee per week, or a fee, paid monthly, that covers the entire mowing season. Instead, they will expect a very low, per-hour rate, often at or below the minimum wage.

Do not feel guilty about making money on your jobs. Avoid bargaining with potential customers. It is a no-win situation for you. Set your pricing at margins you need to keep your business financially healthy and stick to them. If you chose to offer discounts for bundled services or large projects, make it clear that the discount is solely for the bundle or size of the job. If you chose to pursue commercial contracts it is wise to start small and work your way to larger jobs. You can ruin your reputation in the commercial community quickly if you take on a job you cannot fulfill because it is beyond your ability. Network with business professionals who may need your services to get to know them and establish relationships.

For bigger landscaping jobs

It is unlikely that you will want to offer a flat fee for more extensive landscaping work. It is possible to stand back, look at a small yard for a few minutes, and based on previous experience say, "I will charge you $40 to mow your yard," but if your services include planting, weeding, shrub or tree maintenance, fertilizing, designing flower gardens, or providing yard ornamentation, the pricing calculation will probably take some time to figure out. Take the time you need. Customers understand it takes a day or two to get a detailed estimate on a job.

Whatever you do, be sure to itemize all the different areas of labor involved, add in the cost of the products you will be using plus a fair markup on your cost, and your business overhead charges plus your profit. Again, as a startup, you will be wise to track the amount of time it takes to plant a tree or shrub, to weed a garden, or to clip a hedge. Get in the habit of jotting down the time of day when you start a particular part of a project, and again, after it is complete. If you keep careful records, your pricing skills will improve rapidly.

For time and materials

Certain jobs lend themselves to the simpler approach of Time and Materials, or "T&M" costing. Using this method, the landscaper presents an hourly rate, and a standard markup for materials. Sometimes the customer pays the materials cost up-front. Some T&M agreements include a clause "not to exceed X-dollars." This clause eases the customer's mind, by providing is an upper limit to the job, as well as a chance to pay less than the top stated price. Your business overhead costs should be built into your hourly rate. Clear communicating with the customer is essential here, as well. Unless you explain to your customer that you will be billing for time when you are out at the lumberyard picking up fence rails, that customer might believe that if you are not on their property you are not working. Make sure they understand this is not the case.

Do not assume your customers will remember everything you discuss with them. Write it all down and use detailed notes when you bid on business and offer contracts to your customers. There is no need to hand over 60-page documents with lots of small print, but customers appreciate clear definitions and descriptions of the work you will be doing. The bid itself should be easily understood and leave nothing to chance or misinterpretation. If you and your customer review five plans for garden service, document the specifics of the chosen plan so details from the other plans are accidentally recalled. Without a detailed agreement the customer may think he or she told you to build a flowerbed that was actually discussed in a different plan. Avoid side deals in which you offer informal free services with a wink. You might forget the wink, but your customer will not. If you do make special arrangements or include a bonus, add a little note to yourself on your copy of the contact so you will remember you promised a "free weeding of the back flower bed."

There is a temptation once you have done repeated bids for similar projects, to skip the details on future jobs that seem "just the same." For example, you might charge by the square foot for certain services, a method known as unit pricing. It may seem to be easier, but it can be risky to price by the square foot instead of going through a detailed analysis of the work involved. You may save yourself some time with a calculator and notepad, but find yourself in the end, charging too little. If you decide to try this method, start off with just one or two projects. Consider them "experiments" where you go back to double-check time and expenditures after completing a unit-price job. If your first few unit-pricing experiments make the profit you expect, then you are probably safe to continue. But every now and then, step back to evaluate whether you are still making money.

These are just a few basic considerations to determine costs and pricing. There are many other approaches to the bidding process, some involving complicated formulas and meetings with your accountant. How you chose to determine your costs and thus your bids is up to you. Just remember the importance of having accurate base numbers against which you price your services.

CASE STUDY: KELLY'S GREENSCAPES LLC, SHAWN KELLY

Kelly's Greenscapes LLC
W232 N6575 Waukesha Avenue
Sussex, WI 53089
414-617-7443
www.kellysgreenscapes.com

Shawn Kelly originally got into the landscaping business with the intention of paying for guitar lessons. "I started mowing lawns when I was about 12 with my parents' lawn mower," he said. "By the time I was a junior and senior in high school, I had a couple employees." In college, Kelly decided to stay in the field because of the income he knew he could make, and he got a horticultural degree. His LLC is now in its 11th year.

Kelly believes his schooling was a good idea — in part. The college had capable staff to teach about plant life, but the construction training was lacking. "We were given a book geared more toward landscapes in California," he said. "Living in Wisconsin, that's not much help with weather-related issues like freezing and thawing. For that, it is better to learn on the job."

Pricing a mowing job is the same. "You can't give it 25 minutes to calculate. You have to learn how to drive into someone's yard, take a look, and say it will cost $X. Then drive away real quick."

Kelly's company was up to 22 trucks before downsized due to the economy. He uses licensed staff for chemical applications. He has crews for lawn maintenance, snow plowing, planting, hardscapes, tree work, and concrete work. Kelly does not use subcontractors. "We don't farm anything out," he said. "It carries your name if you give the reference, and I feel it can adversely affect your business if the job is not done right — unless you have one person that you can religiously contact, and you know that person will come through for you."

For plant material, Kelly works with a few different nursery suppliers, using some for particular products, and others who offer better pricing for bulk purchases. Much of his business savvy comes through experience. "Nobody in this business comes in knowing everything," he said, citing patio stone installation as an example. "They used to use a sand base. Now they use very finely crushed gravel because it holds up bet ter." Concrete chemical composition has changed; even plants are more disease resistant, thanks to scientists.

Most of Kelly's business comes by word of mouth, though Home and Garden conventions have brought in some good clients. "One thing we thrive on in this business is learning different things from people," he said.

CASE STUDY: KELLY'S GREENSCAPES LLC, SHAWN KELLY

He gets new design ideas at the Home and Garden shows, just as customers do.

Design is an important aspect of his work. "Whenever we do a landscape job, the first thing we discuss is having a landscape design drawn up by our designer — because then the customer knows what they will get for their money," said Kelly. "If everyone bids on the same design, you are comparing apples to apples. But if a customer says 'I want a patio here and this and this,' to five landscapers, those five different landscapers will give five different prices."

Right now, the market is polluted with people who bought lawnmowers and pickup trucks and think they can become arborists, Kelly said. But the biggest challenge in the business is keeping customers happy and getting paid on time, he said. There is just no pleasing some people, even those who live in big, expensive houses. "Every season I have 20 people who try to get the job done as cheap as they can and aren't happy no matter what you do," he said. "The same season, there are people who are thankful for everything you do and respect that you are doing what their budget has afforded."

SECTION FOUR
In the Office

Chapter Nine

Locating Your Office

As a landscaping or yard work professional, you will need a base of operations. If you have multiple vehicles, trucks, trailers, and other large pieces of equipment, you will probably need a garage or other facility where they can be stored and worked on. However, even if you rent a facility to house your equipment, you may keep your actual office somewhere else — such as a spare room in your home.

Home or Facility, Pros and Cons

More than half of America's small businesses are home-based, according to the Small Business Administration. A home office is ideal for a landscaping business, providing you have space for it and your community allows home-based businesses.

Let us examine the zoning issue first. Many communities have restrictions on businesses based in private homes, mostly because of the traffic and other issues associated with operating a business. Check your local zoning. You can do a Web search for your local government or look up the number in the phonebook. Explain what you plan to do. You may be required to pay a license fee. Be aware that your business will have an impact on your neighborhood if you park a truck that says "Lance's Lawn Care" where everyone can see it. If you live in a suburb, you will have a trailer, big pieces of equipment, and employees coming and going — it is not reasonable to operate from a residence. One compromise would be to have your office at home, but rent a storage space for your equipment.

Assuming it is legal for you to base your business at home, why would you want to? For starters, the commute is great. Plus, you always can do the laundry while you are catching up on paper-work. You do not have to pay rent, and there can be some tax benefits too. The Internal Revenue Service has strict guidelines for claiming a home office as a business expense, so discuss the details with your accountant.

While the flexibility of moving around or working whatever hours you would like can be nice, if your office is just down the hall from your kitchen, you never leave work. If a customer calls with a question at 9 p.m., it is tempting to take the call and run to your of-fice for a quick look at whatever the customer is concerned about. Of course, you always can ignore the phone, but the thought of a paying customer is a motivating factor to answer it.

Some other home-office matters to consider are family, friends, and possibly a landlord. Kids may have trouble understanding that you do not have time to play with them or drive them to the mall. Friends may assume that working at home is the same as not working at all, so they drop by to hang out next to your desk. If you rent your home, be sure to inform your landlord about your plans to set up a business there. You do not want to be evicted two weeks after you order letterhead that has your address on it.

CASE STUDY: A.M. SERVICES, MARK FOSTER

A.M. Services
3460 East Ellsworth Road
Ann Arbor, MI 48108
734-973-0930
http://www.am-services-inc.com

Mark Foster started A.M. Snowplow from his dorm room at the University of Michigan in 1975 by borrowing startup money from his father. Today, the company is known as A.M. Services and provides lawn care and snow removal services to hundreds of customers in the Ann Arbor area.

A.M. Services is an S-Corp. and is licensed for pesticide applications, although Foster no longer provides such chemical services to his customers. He does offer pre-emergent fertilizers for his lawn customers.

A.M. Services is strictly a lawn-maintenance company in the summer and a snow-removal service in the winter. During the peak summer season, Mark has about 30 people on his payroll. He provides training during his weekly staff meetings and mixes new employees with his veterans to provide on-the-job training.

Foster's customers have a choice of contracts: seasonal or pay-as-you-go. Seasonal customers receive a discount for lawn maintenance during summer months if they pay the full amount at the beginning of the season. Snow removal customers are offered a choice of a full-season price that remains fixed whether snowfall is heavy or light, or a retainer agreement that covers seven snow removal services with pay-as-you-go fees once the retainer number has been exceeded.

Foster's pricing is based on his company's needs. How big is the yard or driveway? How long will it take to complete the mowing or plowing? How much profit do we need? "Our prices are not based on what others are charging," he says. His pricing and services work for him — he has about 500 customers, summer and winter.

Most of Foster's leads come from referrals, proving that happy customers are the best form of marketing. A.M. Services dropped its yellow pages advertising because the leads the ads were generating were not in line with the business's needs. Foster has tried direct mail and says it generated good leads. He occasionally drops fliers in neighborhoods where he already has business. His trucks also look professional, with lettering on all sides to promote his business.

CASE STUDY: A.M. SERVICES, MARK FOSTER

He targets older neighborhoods where houses are modest and lots are small. His customers are older people who do not want to cut their own grass, and two-income households where the homeowners do not have the time to take care of the yard.

Chapter Ten

Buying Office Equipment and Supplies

Setting Up Your Office

If you are planning to operate your business from home, you will need cooperation. Explain to your family that you are going to need to reserve a room; then, plan your workspace. Make sure it is large enough to be comfortable and efficient for everything you will do there, including contacting vendors and garden design, as well as the day-to-day aspects of marketing, scheduling, payroll, and more. A tiny desk in a corner will not do. You will need space for a large desk, file cabinets, a computer, a printer, possibly a drafting table, at least two chairs, and an area to spread out plans and proposals. You may want to set up an extra place for an assistant to answer the phones or do bookkeeping when you are out. You will need at least a small bookcase. Look to the future. Will you still have room to run your business in that space in a year?

Choose a quiet spot. You cannot work well if there are kids yelling, trains going by, dogs barking, and a television in the background. You will not present a professional appearance if a customer has to ask, "What's that noise?". You will not be giving your business the attention and focus it needs if you are distracted.

Another advantage about running your business from home is the office décor. You will not need to spend big money on a desk or office furniture. Chances are, your customers will not be coming to your home because you will be going to theirs, so an unfinished door or a sheet of plywood for a desktop is acceptable. You can use inexpensive file cabinets to hold it up. Presto: a desk. You also can use a trimmed piece of plywood as a drafting table, supported by blocks or sawhorses. The idea is to have a workspace you can use and that meets your needs. Of course, you want it to be orderly and efficient, but you do not need mahogany at this point.

Phone

While you can start a business with no more than the above essentials, you will probably do better with a few extras. If you want to be listed in the yellow pages, you will need to have a phone dedicated to business. Some people only use a cell phone, but the dedicated line is preferable. It is more expensive, but you can also receive faxes this way. Use the landline telephone as your official business telephone number and forward calls to your cell phone or an answering machine or service. You also will need a fax machine and possibly a dedicated fax line, which can double as a second business line for calls if necessary. If you choose to use your cell phone as your primary business number, you may regret it when your phone rings constantly at job sites. An answering machine on an office line can be accessed remotely, so you will always be able to check your messages, even from job sites.

A two-line business phone is not a luxury. Line one is typically designated as the primary business line. Line two can be assigned as the fax line, and also used to make outgoing calls. Some phone companies offer a "distinctive ring" feature that rings differently if a fax is coming in, so you do not make a mistake and pick up the phone. Telephone prices vary according to quality and features. Find the best one you can afford. Consider models with caller ID and automatic dialing. If you do not plan to use an answering service, consider a telephone with a built-in answering device. Callers will leave messages for you and the device will tell you when they called, so you can prioritize your call returns. You can save yourself some neck discomfort with frequent calls by getting a headset.

Fax machine, copier, and scanner

Unless you plan to use your local copy store for faxes, you will need a fax machine. All-in-one machines are used by many small businesses for faxing, copying, and scanning. The prices are reasonable and they work well. The more-expensive models have extra features and may be more durable. These are inkjet printers, not laser machines, which cost significantly more money. Day-to-day landscape operations can get along quite well with an all-in-one printer, fax, and scanner device.

Calculator

You will need at least two. Your office should have a desktop calculator. They are easier to use, have larger number pads, provide printouts of your calculations, and have features needed for working up bids, such as mark up/mark down. Attach the printouts to your office copy of bids as a way to check your base numbers later in the bidding process. If you add a zero or two in your calculations, it is nice to know where the problem was. The second calculator can be a small pocket model, cell phone or PDA that you will use in the field for quick bids, balances, and other calculating needs.

Digital camera

Unless you are strictly limited to lawn maintenance, you will be executing some great landscape work. Make sure you document it, before and after your work, with a digital camera. Digital photos can be taken at various stages while the work is in process. You may want to print out a set of pictures for your customer, too. If you reduce their size, the best photos can be posted on your Web site as an online portfolio, in addition to the hard-copy portfolio you will compile. Use your hard-copy portfolio in your marketing and bidding process, and at garden shows to bring in new business, and as a resource file for advertising photos.

Postage meter

This is an optional piece of equipment that you lease. How much surface mailing will you do? If you are just going to be sending out a few pieces of mail every month to pay bills or send letters, you may not need one. If you are going to be sending out mass mailings to potential customers as part of your marketing, a postage machine might be a wise choice. If you guess on postage for things bigger than a letter, it is likely you will overpay. A scale and meter combination will give you an exact postage amount and can print out a stamp, just like the post office. Meters pay off only if you do enough mailings to offset the cost of leasing the machine, which varies according to features.

You can also order postage online from **www.usps.com** or download postage from the Web site to your computer, through the new services described here: **www.usps.com/onlinepostage/welcome. htm?from=home_postageoptions&page=onlinepostage**

Point of sale equipment

Credit card processing devices are also known as or point of sale (POS) machines. As with other office items, a wide range of features and prices are available. Some machines provide receipts; others require a separate printer. Receipts are mandatory, one way or another. Some credit card machines are totally portable and can be used at a customer's home. All that is required is an AC electric outlet and a phone plug. There are other, more expensive credit card devices that use cell phone technology, so you can just swipe the card anywhere, enter the price information, and make the charge. POS software is also available. It works with your computer and costs less than a dedicated credit card machine, but you cannot take it with you if you use a desktop computer and your receipt will come from your printer. This type of POS system is often used at doctors' offices and other professional outlets.

Many companies will want your credit card business. Talk to your bank and check the Internet for credit card service companies. Get the best rate you can, because the fees will come out of your company's profit. Credit card service companies and banks typically charge from something more than one percent to as much as three or four percent per transaction. They may tack on monthly "service fees" and other charges. Shop around and negotiate. Be sure to ask the most important questions: How long will it take for your account to be credited with the sale? How often and when will your account be updated? Keep your credit card receipts in your bookkeeping files for later reference if a question should arise. Mistakes can occur. You will want to have backup readily available to reinforce your side of the story.

Office supplies

Standard office supplies include letterheads, envelopes, business cards, and printer ink cartridges. Let us consider the letterhead first. You want a professional look that features your company's name, telephone number, fax number, and your address. If you are working out of your home, and do not feel comfortable revealing this to customers, you may prefer to use a post office box for your business mail. You will want a return address where people can safely send payments. If you want a logo or something beyond basic type, you may wish to have a graphic designer create something simple, professional, and easy to read. You can also choose a tasteful sample from a quick-printer's sample book. There are templates in most word processing programs that can be adapted for your needs as well. This method allows you to print a basic letterhead on your own computer.

Envelopes should reflect your letterhead in style and tone. Use business-sized envelopes (Number 10s). If you decide to include a return envelope, it should be a Number 9, to fit inside with your statement.

A Number 10 envelope will accept standard letterhead, folded horizontally in thirds. There are two types: window and closed envelopes. Window envelopes are frequently used by businesses because the mailing address of the intended party on the inside form shows through the envelope's window. Closed envelopes require that the address of the recipient be separately posted, either by printing it on the envelope or using a pre-printed sticker. If you decide not to have envelopes printed, and do not want to run them through your computer printer, you can either print labels with your return address, or purchase a rubber stamp. When you buy rubber stamps, consider getting one imprinted with "For Deposit Only" and your bank account number, to protect checks from being forged if they are inadvertently lost or stolen before you take them to the bank.

Business cards are essential. You will pass them around to virtually everyone you meet; potential customers are everywhere. The clerk who sells you your letterhead may need his yard maintained; maybe his brother-in-law needs some mulch. The woman at the bank who sets up your account might need some trees planted. You never know when a customer will walk into your life. Business cards should be easy to read. There is nothing more irritating than staring at a business card that has so much information you cannot find the number to call or the service being offered. The card should state your company's name, your name and title, a primary phone number, fax number, e-mail address, and possibly your cell number. As you can see, the card is already busy with just the basics. A simple logo, or none at all, is fine. Get the cards professionally printed to give them a professional appearance. You can go to one of the office supply or chain printers for cards, letterhead, and other such items at a reasonable cost. You also may find companies on the Internet that will offer quick turnaround at low prices for such products.

You may also want pre-printed invoices, estimate sheets, and service lists. It is acceptable to print these yourself on your computer as long as they look professional.

Computers and Software

Personal Computers (PCs) based on IBM's original model and Apple Macintosh Computers (Macs) and their variants are both fine for your business. Macs may be less virus-prone, though that is changing. They are considered very reliable, but also more expensive and have fewer specialty business software programs designed to work with them because there are fewer Macs in businesses.

PCs are often less expensive and have thousands of software programs available for them, and more brands to choose from, so you can do more shopping around. The price of PCs has come down so much it would be hard to justify purchasing a used one. Some new PCs are in the $500 range, including a monitor. Do not forget that whatever you buy will probably be out of date in a couple of years.

Your first consideration is what you need to make your business run. You are going to access the Internet, probably with a cable, wireless, or DSL broadband connection, so you will need speed and power for that.

You will be downloading and processing photo files, so you need a large hard drive to store the photos. You will need Adobe Photoshop TM or other photo processing software and probably a scanner, as well as a color printer, either inkjet or laser.

Most likely you will be keeping your books on the computer, processing orders, maintaining files, creating spreadsheets, faxing, storing, and printing. If you are in the landscaping or landscape architecture business, you will be using landscaping software, possibly even computer-assisted drafting (CAD) programs, drafting, credit card processing, and many other tasks specifically related to your business.

Explain your needs to the computer companies or retailers you are dealing with and compare their responses. If you have friends or family members who are more computer savvy than you are, ask them for their advice.

Desktop or laptop?

Both options have benefits and drawbacks. The desktop computer probably will have a bigger screen and an easy-to-use-keyboard, and external devices such as your printer and modem usually are plugged in. A desktop may cost less than a laptop. But, you cannot take it into the field to use for presentations and proposals. A laptop is portable and easy to use, but it costs more. The cheapest route is to select the most powerful desktop you can afford to get the most computing power for your money. You can purchase a laptop when your business has grown and you have more cash to spend.

You may want to purchase an external hard drive to back up or archive your document files and other essential records at least once a week to avoid data catastrophes. Back up or copy in an archive all important data, such as designs, invoices, and your financial records at least daily or every time you work on a file.

You may also want to consider an online-backup system, in addition to backing up your computer locally to an external hard drive. Two reasonably-priced options are offered by **www.mozy. com** and **www.ibackup.com** . Regular backups protect your data from electrical blackouts, viruses, and other calamities.

Business software

Your new computer will come with the software necessary to operate, whether it is a PC or Mac. It probably will come with a word processing program, Internet browser, an e-mail program, and other programs that the manufacturer includes with the initial purchase.

PCs often come with Microsoft Office, an office suite that includes MS Word, Excel, PowerPoint, and Internet Explorer. Macs come with the Mac word processing program, but work well with Microsoft products. There are many other word processing programs, some of them free (check at **www.openoffice.com** for samples). Realistically, at this time, it is a Microsoft world in business and if you want to easily transfer files to other companies for bids and proposals, you can assume they want them in MS Word. Beware of word-processing or other programs whose functionality is limited.

Computer Security

Firewalls and virus protection programs are essential tools in computer protection. European Union computer security experts estimated in 2007 that viruses begin to attack new computers on the Internet within seconds. Firewalls — whether hardware, software, or a combination of the two — protect your computer from unwelcome intrusions.

Virus protection programs protect your computer against specific, known viruses. Symantec, McAfee, and Norton are among the best-known software providers of this type of protection. Their programs must be updated regularly — preferably every day — to guard against the latest viruses, so you will want a renewable subscription, less than $100 annually for the basics.

If you are already familiar with computers, you are probably conscious of spammers, who send out millions of e-mail messages for products or services you have never requested, and the "phishing" schemes they pursue. If not, you need to know that dishonest computer hackers constantly try to steal your passwords, bank account numbers, and other personal or business identity information to steal your money or your identity. The simplest way to protect yourself is to never click a link sent by someone you do not know, especially if the person claims to be a "webmaster" at a bank, your Internet service provider, or some other legitimate-sounding source. If you are doubtful, phone the company that is supposedly requesting the information from you. You want to make sure you have every resource available to help protect your computer against the latest schemes of hackers who want to access your bank accounts, credit cards, passwords, and all of the other information you need to protect.

Accounting Software

There are numerous brands of accounting software. Some are so popular that other software providers create "add-ons" that improve the functionality of the software. Again, there are many choices and you should work with your accountant to coordinate bookkeeping with her or him.

QuickBooks, which was mentioned earlier, is one of the most widely used programs. It is offered in both PC and Mac versions. There are small-business versions that allow you to balance your checkbook, do your payroll, track expenses by category, and create custom forms. You will want to discuss *all* of the accounting details of your business with your accountant *before* you set up your books so you will all be on the same page. There are many accounting terms that he or she may use that you might not understand, for example: "Are you on an accrual or cash basis?" QuickBooks takes a little practice to use effectively, but it is not difficult if you take an hour or two to get the basics, set up accounts, and gain some understanding of what it does. QuickBooks offers a contractor edition that allows you to track job costs and profits and to manage progress on several jobs at once.

However, QuickBooks is not the only highly rated business accounting program available. Peachtree, Microsoft Money, MYOB Business Essentials, NetSuite Small Business Accounting, and Simply Accounting Pro are others. They will all provide the basic features you need to run your business, and they offer special features besides helping to balance your checkbook and calculate payroll taxes. They offer sophisticated business applications that can help you grow your business into more than an entity that cuts grass.

Once you have a good accounting program and have categories set up correctly, you will not need your accountant every day. Instead your accountant can do weekly, monthly, or even quarterly oversight and monitoring. If you do not enjoy working with the figures, you may choose to hire a part-time bookkeeper to maintain the numbers and perform data entry. However, if you hire someone else to oversee your financial resources check the records periodically to be sure everything adds up, or ask your accountant to review your employee's work if you do not understand it. Companies of every size have had to grapple with misuse of funds or embezzlement. The best way to prevent this is to keep monitoring the books, or have someone you trust do it for you.

Obviously, you will want to start your business financial dealings by using a separate business bank account. It is confusing and risky to co-mingle your personal funds with the business resources. Maintain a business checking account under the business name. Deposit all business checks into that account. Have credit card payments deposited there. If a customer pays you cash, deposit the money into the business account. If you are operating as a sole proprietorship, and need to pay yourself for the work you have performed, write a check from the business account to yourself, then deposit it into your personal account. Run your business squeaky clean today to avoid nasty problems tomorrow. Here are some basic accounting terms you may want to discuss with your accountant — together you can decide what will work best for your particular situation:

Cash versus accrual. The cash method is recording a sale when the money is received and an expense recorded when the cash goes out. This measures only what happens in your business, not necessarily when you made the sale. Accrual is recording the income when you invoice the job and recording expenses when they are incurred, not when they are paid.

Double entry versus single entry. Double means every one of your business entries is registered twice: once as a debit, once as a credit. You must be sure that everything balances — dollars are recorded coming in and going out. Single-entry bookkeeping is easier but is more prone to mistakes because there is no automatic balance. Your accountant will probably use the double-entry system.

Debit versus credit. Debit is the payout. Credit is where you got the money. Your company buys a rake. The rake is a debit. The money to pay for the rake is the credit.

Calendar year versus fiscal year. Businesses operate on a 12-month cycle. Theoretically, it can begin at any time of year. If your business operates on a calendar year, that means your annual bookkeeping begins on January 1 and ends December 31. If you operate your business on a fiscal year, it means you begin your 12-month bookkeeping cycle some time after January 1 and end it 12 months after that. For instance, the federal government's fiscal year begins October first. Some business structures, such as sole proprietorships, are required to operate on a calendar year. However, you maintain your books, your business-year structure is important for tax issues and to anchor your annual business planning and assessment.

What we are discussing here is the critical importance of keeping accurate and detailed books. There are lots of terms and systems, but nothing is as important as committing yourself to fine bookkeeping. You must keep track of all accounts, income, and expenses. This is critical to the health and growth of your company. It is the only way you can know how your business is doing and whether you are meeting projections. It is the method by which you will track the effectiveness of your marketing because your record keeping will tell you where your leads come from, what your closing rate is, how much your average customer spends, what services they need (and request), what your materials cost, how much you pay your employees, and all of the other small and large details of operating a successful landscaping business. Use the best software that offers the most small business support.

Business planning software can assist you in putting your business plan together, as well as plan its growth and future. Palo Alto Software offers something called Business Plan Pro, which provides hundreds of sample business plans as examples and helps you work through the process of putting your own plan together. Plan Writer Deluxe and Ultimate Business Planner are two other options for planning software. HomeOfficeReports. com reviews business-planning software and looks things like ease of use, cost, support, features, and compatible software. The cost of this type of software from is $50 to $1,000, depending on features, sophistication, and other factors. You probably do not need business-planning software that can support a Fortune 500 company. A program that can help you put your business together and plan for growth is adequate. Beware of loading your computer with too many large programs that slow down your operating system. Look over your business planning software options and pick one that meets your needs. Remember, if you are using QuickBooks Pro or another high-quality accounting program, it will contain some of the planning elements you need so you do not need to duplicate these features with another program. For a small, startup business, it is a good idea to keep things simple.

Landscaping or nursery software is specific to your business. As with other software decisions, you have many choices, although none of the outdoor services management software we found was available to run on a Mac. However, if you are a Mac owner and run Parallels software, which allows Windows programs to run on a Mac, these products may work well for you. Here are a few examples of what is available:

Gopher Software (**www.gophersoftware.com**) offers basic, plus, and pro versions. The basic version is for smaller landscaping companies. Gopher Plus is designed for larger companies that want to directly export information to Quickbooks or track expenses for individual jobs. It allows you to do such things as factor late fees and other bookkeeping issues, and Pro expands on it to include chemicals, equipment maintenance scheduling, and more. All Gopher landscaping versions allow you to schedule jobs, track progress on these jobs, schedule work by routes, price jobs, bill jobs, create bids, and estimate and track invoicing aging. Gopher's software links to QuickBooks. Gopher product pricing ranges from about $100 to more than $200.

Groundskeeper (**www.groundskeeperpro.com**) offers three landscape-related software programs: Groundskeeper Pro, Groundskeeper Lite, and Blizzard Buster. Groundskeeper Lite allows you to track up to 10,000 customers, price regular and special services, and provides most of the features that Gopher offers. Groundskeeper Pro expands in the manner of Gopher's Pro version. Blizzard Buster is, as the name implies, for companies that offer snow-removal services. Groundkeeper software is priced from under $300 to about $400.

Tree Management Systems (**www.treemanagement.net**) offers professional landscaping software in ArborGold and TurfGold versions. ArborGold specializes in tree care and management. TurfGold is for lawn care companies. TurfGold and ArborGold are compatible with QuickBooks and MS Office. The company also offers a PhoneCenter program to take calls. TurfGold will help you manage your landscaping business and has special features such as the ability to determine which of your crews is most productive. This may not be something you will need as you start your company, but it could be useful later. TurfGold is $995 and can hold up to 500 different customer's information.

There are also some shareware programs available, like Lawn Manager Pro. It is available for download at several shareware sites. The cost is under $100. As a landscaping professional, you may also want to consider software programs that allow you to draft landscaping design projects on your computer. Computer Assisted Design (CAD) programs allow you to enter the dimensions of the yard or lot you are working with and draft 3D plans. You can show these plans to your customer to give them a better understanding of how their yard or home exterior will look. If they want changes, it is as easy as moving your mouse around. There are many CAD programs available for prices that reflect their features. You can expect to spend more than $1,000 for a top-of-the-line program. A basic CAD program is around $50.

For example, 3D Garden Composer (**www.gardencomposer.com**) is primarily an inexpensive graphics program for landscapers or do-it-yourselfers. It allows you to insert your photographs into a garden plan and manipulate them; it provides an encyclopedia of plants and explains plant diseases. If you are offering nursery or garden design services this program is less than $50 and a good beginning program.

At the other end of the cost spectrum, VizTerra is a 3D design system for professional landscapers and landscape architects. It can do everything, from creating design templates from your drawings to showing your designs under different lighting conditions (based on the various times of day). VizTerra is remarkably detailed, and is available for use on a monthly ($95) or annual license ($995) — not a contract. So if you do not need the program all the time, you do not have to pay a fortune. The site offers a very detailed description and downloadable demo at **www. structurestudios.com/website/vizterra/vizterra.html**.

This list is just a sampling of the many software programs offered for professional landscapers. As you search the Web or talk to other professionals, you will find other programs to look at. Groundskeeper and Gopher get most of the buzz and their reviews are generally positive. To some degree, both are accounting programs, so compatibility with QuickBooks is good because information is shared between the programs.

For the lawn care or nursery business management software, look for features like these:

- Compatibility with your accounting software, so you avoid entering all the numbers twice

- Maintain your customer base information such as who they are, what they purchase, and when they get it

- Account history

- Pricing for regular and special services and products

- Rates

- Special fees

- Materials pricing

- Print bills

- Track payments

- Job estimates and proposals

- Contract forms for residential and commercial accounts

- Marketing and lead tracking

- Suppliers and vendors history and pricing

- Calendars for jobs, seasons, and marketing

You may add or subtract items from this list according to your needs and the features you find in your accounting software, which may duplicate some of the above. The goal here is to help you manage your landscaping services business. Do not buy software features you do not need, and do not pass up important features simply to get a cheaper price.

Ideally, you will have software that allows you to sit down, open it up, and see everything you have scheduled for that day and the status of projects you have bid on, contracted, begun, and finished. It also should tell you who owes you money and to whom you owe money, how much, and its status. In short, it tells you where you are in your business. It will be much easier to run your business if you are not digging around on a cluttered desk looking for key documents such as your schedule of jobs.

Some Web sites to check for software that is specifically designed for landscape professionals include:

- CompuScapes (**www.compuscapes.com**) software management solutions for the green industry

- Design Imaging Group (**www.designimaginggroup.com/landscape.cfm**)

- LM Software (**www.lawnmonkey.com**) schedule software

- Qxpress (**www.qxpress.com**) offers an add-on for Quick-Books for landscapers

- Slice Technologies (**www.sliceplus.com**) software for nurseries and retail garden centers

- UDS Green Industry Software Inc. (**www.udsgis.com**) customized for green industry businesses from ten users or less to major corporations.

Bookkeeping

We are fortunate to be living in a time of computerized accounting programs which make estimating prices, sending invoices, paying bills, writing checks, and keeping financial records a far easier task than dealing with old-fashioned paper ledgers. If you are not sure which program to buy, your accountant can guide you in choosing accounting software that works with your computer. He or she will explain the preferred system of accounting for you to use, whether cash or accrual. If you have decided to do your own recordkeeping and do not want to use an accountant, QuickBooks is relatively easy to use and reasonably priced, available at **www.intuit.com**. It will help you organize your vendors and customers, track delinquent payments, and automatically recall previous statements among many other features.

No matter what software program you choose, you or an assistant will have to regularly enter all the financial records. Do not let financial data pile up on the desk. There is nothing worse than being forced to enter three months of neglected financial data just before tax time, or reconcile several belated bank statements one after the other. You might even lose track of an invoice, forget to bill a customer, and never be paid.

Hiring Office Help

After your business is underway and you start going out to quote jobs or work in the field, you may decide that a phone answering machine is not enough. There are definite advantages in having someone in the office to answer the phones, call the vendors, and do phone marketing or set schedules for bidding. Some of this work cannot wait until dark when the outside jobs are done.

You may want to tiptoe into the role of employing an office worker. Part-time help is easy to come by in today's economy. You may simply ask around among friends or relatives. Or, if you are reluctant to take a chance on a friend's recommendation, and you live in an urban or suburban area, place a classified ad in your local paper or online publication, or on a local/national site such as Craigslist.org or Monster.com. You will probably receive more job applications than you can handle.

Start the selection process before you place the ad by describing exactly what you want this employee to do, what experience he or she will need before starting, and what software programs or equipment skills the person will need to have. Also remember that your office helper may well become the "face and voice" of your business. So the person you choose should be able to get along with the public, in person and especially on the phone. You may want someone who can also do cold calling to solicit business for an extra bonus if an appointment is actually set. Or, perhaps you would rather have a bookkeeper to take over some of the data entry responsibilities. Whatever it is you want, write it down, read it over several times, and picture the kind of person you would feel comfortable with. Personality counts. You know who you can and cannot get along with. If your office is in your home, this person will be in your home too, so your family will also have to find your employee a congenial presence in their lives.

Once you place the ad and the applications roll in, make sure you keep all the "possible" job applicant letters you receive. The first person you hire may not work out. If that happens, you will have the stack of letters sitting there, and can contact some others on your list. It is polite, if possible, to notify those you turn down that they were not accepted, and thank them for their application. You want to be polite with everyone you come in contact with, because you will never know if that job applicant is the son, daughter, or cousin of a current or potential customer. Besides, getting in the habit of being polite to everyone pays off over time.

When you interview the applicants, note their personality and how comfortable you feel with them in the room. Go down your checklist of job requirements to see how they fit. Be careful to avoid certain personal questions, such as age, whether or not the person is married, has children, or their religion. The federal government posts a general description of what you legally cannot ask a potential employee at **www.eeoc.gov/facts/qanda.html**

The following excerpt from that site will give you an idea of what to avoid doing or saying to stay in compliance with federal law:

Discriminatory practices

Under Title VII, the ADA, and the ADEA, it is illegal to discriminate in any aspect of employment, including:

- Hiring and firing

- Compensation, assignment, or classification of employees

- Transfer, promotion, layoff, or recall

- Job advertisements

- Recruitment

- Testing

- Use of company facilities

- Training and apprenticeship programs

- Fringe benefits

- Pay, retirement plans, and disability leave

- Other terms and conditions of employment.

Discriminatory practices under these laws also include:

- Harassment on the basis of race, color, religion, sex, national origin, disability, or age.

- Retaliation against an individual for filing a charge of discrimination, participating in an investigation, or opposing discriminatory practices.

- Employment decisions based on stereotypes or assumptions about the abilities, traits, or performance of individuals of a certain sex, race, age, religion, or ethnic group, or individuals with disabilities.

- Denying employment opportunities to a person because of marriage to, or association with, an individual of a particular race, religion, national origin, or an individual with a disability. Title VII also prohibits discrimination because of participation in schools or places of worship associated with a particular racial, ethnic, or religious group.

Employers are required to post notices to all employees advising them of their rights under the laws that EEOC enforces and their right to be free from retaliation. Such notices must be accessible to persons with visual or other disabilities that affect reading.

These guidelines should be followed by all business people, even small, start-up businesses like yours.

Once you select a person to hire, you will need to set up a personnel file for him or her, prepare the appropriate government paperwork for tax withholding, and other new-hire policies. If you are not sure what is required, your accountant, your state tax officer, or your local chamber of commerce can point you in the right direction.

You will also want to set aside some concentrated time to train your new employee in the way you want the business to be handled. He or she may be spending a lot of "alone time" in the office if you are out in the field. You will want to closely monitor the results of the office work you assign to be sure the job is done. With any luck, there will be no problems, but if there are you will have to retrain or fire the individual. Neither of these tasks is much fun; it is much easier to pick your employee carefully from the start.

Finally, since you hired an office worker to take the burden off yourself, you will want to see some payback in terms of increased revenue within a fairly short period of time. Be sure you do a cost analysis of your hiring experiment to see if it is bringing you more income, or costing you more money than you expected.

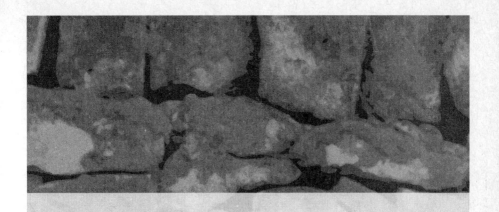

SECTION FIVE
In The Field

Chapter Eleven

Buying Professional Equipment and Supplies

Outdoor Equipment

First, because you are serious about this business, you already know you want professional-level equipment, so buy the best you can afford. In the long run, it will be cheaper than the low-quality, or heavily used equipment that turns up on sale in the paper or online. You want equipment that will stand up to the demands of a professional landscaping business and will not need to be replaced after only a few months on the job.

Your truck

Lawn care specialists do not stuff a lawnmower into the trunk of the family car. Acquire a vehicle that can haul your mower(s), edgers, hedge cutters, rakes, seeders, shovels, snowblowers, pruning gear, and all of the other items you will be using in your business, as well as a few cubic yards of mulch and topsoil. You will need at least a full-sized pickup or van. If you want to consider more heavy-duty work, you might look into getting a one-ton flatbed. These trucks are regularly seen around town hauling landscaping equipment and dirt. They are bigger than a pickup and are built to carry heavier loads. The most important characteristic of your business vehicle is its ability to meet your basic business needs, not your aesthetic needs. You need hauling ability, not luxury. If you live in an area that experiences severe winters and will be offering snow-removal services, you can make a good winter income with a plow. That requires a vehicle that can handle one, and operates with four-wheel drive.

Look for deals. Check online vehicle sale sites and newspapers. Call vehicle rental companies to ask about vehicles coming off lease or rental programs. You can save a significant amount of money by purchasing a used vehicle. Before you buy, however, take it to a mechanic you trust to get an independent assessment of its mechanical soundness. You need reliability. It will not help your business if you have to cancel appointments because your truck will not start.

Trailers

You probably have seen landscapers hauling equipment on trailers. The trailers provide extra carrying capacity and can be used for specific needs such as large mowers or loads of topsoil or mulch. Some landscaping companies leave equipment on the trailers at night.

Trailers come in two basic types: open and enclosed. Open trailers are lighter and require less fuel to haul around. There are many aftermarket kits that allow you to set up racks and other specialized configurations. They also cost less than fully enclosed trailers. They also are open to the elements, which may be an issue if you receive a two-foot snowfall.

Enclosed trailers have four sides and a roof. It is what it implies: a small, rolling storage room. They are heavier, so they use more fuel and they cost more to purchase. But you can lock them at night with a measure of security for the equipment you keep inside, which also applies on job sites where security is an issue. Trailers vary widely in cost, from a few hundred to a few thousand dollars.

Mowers

A mower is probably the most important individual piece of equipment on your list. There are three basic mower options: push it, walk behind it, or ride it. Push mowers are the most common, especially for homeowner operation. The noisy, stinky machine you pushed under the hot summer sun of your teenage years is still available in all its small, backbreaking glory. But, you will not want to use it for your business, at least not as a primary mower.

If you are going to be mowing, trimming, edging, hauling, and digging all day, you do not want to add to your burdens and time constraints by pushing a small mower back and forth for hours across a large, grassy yard. However, a small push mower may come in quite handy as an alternative in some parts of narrow urban yards. If you decide to purchase a push mower, spend the extra money for a professional model with at least a 21-inch cutting width and at least five horsepower. Unless you are going to be cutting a lot of small yards, use this one as a backup to other, more powerful models.

Self-propelled mowers are worth the extra money. They provide their own forward power so you simply walk behind and guide them. A variable-speed, self-propelled mower allows you to set the pace of the work without feeling as though the machine is dragging you along. All new mowers are required to have a blade brake clutch (BBC). This stops the blade from spinning if you lose control of the mower. One version of the BBC stops the blade and the engine when you release the controls on the handle; the other stops only the blade. The second option allows you to empty the clipping bag or push the mower over walkways and other obstacles without having to restart the engine to resume mowing.

Riding mowers for professionals are not the little tractors suburban dads ride around their yards on Saturdays. Mowers for professionals are designed for rough duty day after day. Professional models have cutting decks up to 60 inches and mid sized models have 15 horsepower or more. If you are going to be doing large lawns or commercial jobs, you will need a large self-propelled or riding mower. Get the largest model you can for the jobs you will be doing. Large, self-propelled models can be turned into riders with optional items called sulkies or velkes. These are trailer-like devices that attach to the mower. You sit on the sulky, or you stand on the velke, while the mower pulls you around as you guide it.

Commercial mowers are available with either fixed or floating decks that support the mowing blade(s). A fixed deck costs less and is attached to the mower in the position you set. Its height does not have to be adjusted for each job site. However, it can scalp bumps in rough or hilly lawns and is more of an issue on the wider models, say 60 inches or so, where you may be cutting a large swath of uneven yard.

A floating deck is suspended from the mower frame and "floats" side to side and back to front over the contours of a lawn, offering a smoother, even cut without those annoying bald spots that make customers want discounts. A floating deck is more expensive than a fixed deck, but it does a higher-quality job.

Reel mowers are more complicated devices that use finely calibrated blades for precise cuts. Reel mowers often are used on golf courses and for high-end customers who want the best cut available. Good reel mowers are expensive and require more care and skill to operate and maintain them. You might want to wait to purchase this item until your business and knowledge grow.

Mower tips

A good professional mower will probably cost at least $1,000. Remember, this is a primary business tool and you do not want to buy cheap equipment. You will need something that will endure rough treatment on a daily basis. Depending on size and options, you could spend more than $10,000 for a top-of-the-line pro model. A midrange or less expensive mower will probably do fine for your first year or two in business.

You will not get a long warranty on a professional mower. Manufacturers know these tools get rough treatment, so they offer shorter warranty periods, sometimes as short as ninety days. Talk to your dealer about any downtime programs that might be available, so you will have a loaner if your machine is in the shop.

It certainly helps to have a knack for fixing machinery yourself. You can save a lot of money if you can handle basic maintenance and repair on your own mowers, trailers, and trucks. You can get years of good service out of a quality mower, but it will need regular maintenance, oil changes, and repairs. It can be expensive to drop off your high-priced pro mower at a repair shop. Learn to fix it yourself by reading the manual and following all maintenance recommendations. Change the oil often. Clean filters. Treat your equipment with the respect it deserves. After all, your equipment keeps you in business by helping you deliver your service and products.

During downtimes or periods of bad weather when you cannot be in the field, check your mowers, blowers, edgers, and other items for wear. Are starter cords fraying? Do they need to be replaced? How do your spark plugs look? Are all of the parts tight? Lubricated? Do not leave your equipment and tools out in the weather. During the mowing season, it is important that you clean your lawn-mower deck regularly and keep the blades sharp. During the busiest part of the year, you may need to sharpen your blade daily. You will need a bench grinder and a tool to remove the blade. Sharpen to the angle of the blade. Remember to remove the spark plug wire before you try to remove the blade to ensure the mower does not start while you are in the deck housing. If the blade is bent, replace it.

Edgers

Line Edgers also are known as weed whackers, weed eaters, line trimmers, and string trimmers. The edger is a device that uses a line or a cord that spins out from the motor. It whirls so fast that it slices vegetation in its path. Choosing an edger is a tradeoff between power and weight. The more power it has, the more it weighs. That is a strong consideration if you are going to be using the device for several hours a day. Commercial edgers weigh about 9 pounds for the lighter models to 12 pounds or more for

the high-power models. If you need the power, think about getting a shoulder harness to help support it.

Some edger models come with curved or flex shafts. Many professional landscapers claim these models are hard on the back
over long work periods, so they favor the straight shaft models.

Edger heads are available in "tap and go" or "smart head" models. Tap and go is the most common style. The spinning lines ex-
tends when the head is tapped on the ground while spinning.
You will need to extend the line occasionally because the ends
wear off with use. The smart head models automatically extend
the line when it senses that the cord is short.

Blade edgers use blades in place of cords. They are used for
heavier-duty jobs such as trimming sidewalks and other areas
that need a clean, sharp edge. Size, power, and weight are issues
to consider when evaluating for purchase.

Snow-removal equipment

If you live in a region that experiences long, snowy winters, think
about offering snow-removal services to keep you busy and funded when you are not cutting lawns and planting flowers. This is
not an issue if you live in Florida, along the Gulf Coast, or in southern California. However, if you live in Minnesota, the Northeast,
or the Rocky Mountain region, snow removal is a normal part of
landscaping services. To offer professional-grade snow removal,
you will need more than a few snow shovels. You will need two
expensive pieces of equipment: a snowplow and a snow blower.
You may find deals on used equipment that will bring the cost
down. If you are going to offer this service, you must have a truck

that can handle the plow. Plow and blade styles vary according to the size of the truck. You probably will not be plowing interstate highways so you will not need a very large truck, but you may be plowing parking lots and private community streets, so consider the size of the job when you look for equipment. A snow blower is great for sidewalks and small driveways. You will still need the snow shovels for tight spots and finish work. Look around and get a lightweight metal shovel that is easy on the back.

Other useful power equipment

Blowers can be used for a number of landscaping tasks, most often to blow grass clippings off sidewalks and driveways. You can save money by using a broom, but if you have the money, get a blower. The more powerful models are worn on the body in backpack style, and can be used for leaf blowing in the fall. Again, there is the tradeoff of power, weight, and price. Get the best and most comfortable you can afford.

Power trimmers are useful if you are offering more than simple lawn maintenance. Use them to trim bushes, hedges, and other shrubs. They come with single- or double-sided blades, ranging from 18 to 40 inches long. Unless you have some skill with this piece of equipment, start with a smaller model.

Power rakes are used to dethatch lawns. They are also called vertical mowers. You can get one as an attachment to your lawn mower or as an independent piece of equipment. Power rakes are nice to have, but you probably will not need one when your business is still in its infancy.

Other useful power equipment, depending on the services you plan to offer, include chain saws, pole saws, power washers, and garden tillers.

Non-power hand tools and other items

Having the proper tools is the best way to get any job done. As a landscaper, you will need professional-quality basic yard and garden implements. You might consider a large box to store them so they will not be scattered all over your truck, trailer, or storage area. Here is a basic list:

- Shovels, pointed and square edged. At least one set per crew.
- Spade
- Cultivating fork
- Hoe
- Pick
- Wheel barrow (contractor grade)
- Hand truck
- Tarps
- Large plastic trash can
- Leaf and bow rakes
- Heavy duty hoses, nozzles, sprinkler, and watering can
- Sledgehammer (for driving stakes)
- Eight-foot ladder
- Tree saw (for removing small branches, and so forth)
- Small garden tools for digging and weeding

- Sighting level (to measure elevations and grades)
- Measuring wheel (for accurate dimensions)

In addition to all of the above, you will need high-quality leather work gloves to protect your hands from all of the tools listed above, steel-toed work boots, and a hat to keep the sun off your face. Everyone who works for you also should have gloves, good boots, a hat, and safety glasses to protect them from debris flying around from the power tools they will be using. Ear protection from the noise of loud power tools also is a good idea.

What Does All of This Cost?

The answer is, it depends. If you buy everything new at full retail, the tools alone could run you $8,000 to $10,000, and that is if you stay away from the top-of-the-line power mowers. If you have patience, shop around, and are willing to purchase used equipment, you can save significant amounts of money. Your truck will be the most expensive piece of equipment you will purchase — $15,000 is a good starting point for a decent used truck. Think of it as an investment, not an expense. It will make you money.

Pricing all of this will require you to do some homework. Quality trumps price every time. Meaning, the best equipment, if well maintained, will ultimately be lower cost than unreliable cheap equipment that needs to be replaced often. The equipment we have listed here is the heart of your business. It is better to start small with quality service and equipment than to try to start big with bargain equipment and so-so service to customers. Your business is much better served by a small list of happy customers than a long list of unhappy ones.

Essential Maintenance

Chances are if you are considering an outdoor service business, you already have some maintenance skills. You do not need to be told to keep your tools, mowers, trucks, and other equipment clean and in good working order. The better you maintain your equipment, the longer it will last. It is also true that every time you sharpen your own mower blade, or replace the sparkplugs, change the oil, or even simply clean out the grass and crud from under the mower to keep the airflow lifting the grass blades up for cutting, you save money that a competitor without repair skills will have to spend at the mower shop.

If you are not handy with a wrench and toolkit, or are more a garden-design type of person, you may want to partner with or hire an all-round "fix-it" guy to head up your in-house repair team. This person can teach you or other employees how to keep mowers, trucks, and other gear operating smoothly at a minimal cost. He can also make sure you have equipment properly prepared for storage in the off-season, if you have snowy winters.

A comfortable, orderly workshop will make maintenance more efficient. Set up your workshop in an adequate, dry, and heated space with a solid workbench, vise, and grinder. A heated workshop in climates with winter weather means you can use your off time to rehab mowers, rebuild engines, and get all your working gear in top condition for spring. Purchase a few sturdy floor jacks to support the mowers, tractors, or trucks when you are working on them. Sharpen mower blades daily for a crisp, clean cut. While any good bench grinder can sharpen a blade, you will get a precision edge by investing in a professional blade grinder such as those sold at **www.landscaperpro.com**. Lubricate tools regularly. Tighten nuts and bolts often, because vibration shakes them loose. Minor repairs, such as replacing a wheel or changing and re-gapping spark plugs, do not take years of experience to figure out. Major repairs are a different story. Before you tackle rebuilding even a small engine, or something that sounds simple, like cleaning and readjusting a carburetor, be sure you have the proper instructions at your side and follow them to the letter. Unless you really do know what you are doing and why, you do not want to "experiment" with the equipment that helps you pay for groceries and gasoline.

You will want to keep all your instruction manuals in an easily accessible, central location—not tucked here and there among the oil cans in the shed. Keep all the manuals that come with new equipment. When you buy used machines, ask if the manuals are available. If not, you may be able to find them on the Internet. Check at websites such as **www.repairmanual.com/lawnmowers** or **www. shakyparts.com/manuals.html**. Manufacturers often set up engine-specific web sites, such as **www.briggsandstratton.com/**

It does not matter much whether you keep your manuals filed in the workshop itself, or in your office. All that matters is that you can find them when you need them. If they are in the office, you or your office helper can make calls for repair parts with the part numbers and descriptions right in front of you. Finding a particular tool can take five seconds or five hours, depending on the care with which it was put away the last time it was used. If you start with the goal of keeping your workshop orderly, you will be surprised how employees and family members may pitch in to help you keep it that way.

Outdoor Supplies

Chemicals

There may be no more sensitive issue in America today than the environment. Environmental debate is serious and widespread and virtually every state is reviewing environmental laws and standards. Consequently, it is no longer permissible for a commercial landscape company to grab a bag or two of fertilizer or pesticide and spread it around without regard to federal, state, and local regulations. Are unlicensed people out there doing this? Absolutely. Do you want to be one of them? Not unless you are prepared to pay heavy fines in a society that is increasingly conscious of chemical risk.

Laws and products are constantly changing to meet the environmental challenges we are facing today, so review your state's laws governing the use of chemicals in your work, obtain the necessary training, licenses, and permits, or, find someone who has all of the necessary qualifications and licenses and subcontract your work to him or her. This can be time consuming and distracting for the owner of a new business, but you will forced to either tell potential customers that you do not provide fertilizing, pesticide, and other chemical or organic products, or find a way to deliver these products.

You do not need to feel you are dropping the ball if you do not offer fertilizer, pesticide, or herbicide services. There is no stigma in using subcontractors to perform these tasks. Later in the book there is more discussion of subcontracting, which is an essential part of the lawn and garden service industry. Even large landscaping companies do business this way. It is often more efficient and ultimately less costly to subcontract out the specialized services that would detract you from what you do best. For both your piece of mind and that of your customers, in the case of chemicals, it may be a good idea to leave this sensitive and changing arena to those who know it best.

A Web search of fertilizers and pesticides proves the point: state agriculture departments offer all kinds of information about how and what to use, or not use. For an example, let us review the policies of the state of Maryland. Maryland enforces an aggressive nutrient management program designed to ease pollution of Chesapeake Bay, one of the world's great estuaries. Millions of people live in the bay's drainage area. Runoff from lawns, golf courses, and parks has become a serious problem for the bay and its tributaries. Every landscaping company in Maryland, as well as in Virginia, Delaware, Pennsylvania, and the District of Columbia is, in some way, affected by the regulations put in place to ease the pollution.

The Maryland Department of Agriculture "reviews the fertilizer application records of commercial lawn care companies, as well as non-agricultural nutrient applicators to ensure that nutrients are being applied properly." These words are from a state Web site. They illustrate a couple of important points that apply all across the country. First, note the words "fertilizer application records." This means commercial landscape companies are required to maintain records of their fertilizer applications — records that can be reviewed by state authorities. Second, note the words "applied properly." This means the state has standards for such applications that they expect will be followed. This same Web site advises homeowners to choose a landscaping company "that embraces environmentally sound management practices."

Many other states have similar regulations. The state of Maine restricts the sale of fertilizer containing phosphorous to protect the state's water, and offers help in finding phosphorous-free fertilizers. Iowa bans the dumping of yard wastes, including grass clippings, at landfills unless those landfills offer composting facilities. In California, Florida, Minnesota, and elsewhere across America, state governments are addressing issues of water pollution and other environmental problems caused by products that are used to make lawns greener, bushes fuller, flowers brighter, and trees taller. You owe it to yourself and your business to stay current in your state's requirements for training, as well as its laws and regulations.

There is little room for error here. The state of Maryland site declares "Lawn care companies and commercial landscapers are also required by this law to apply fertilizers in accordance with the most recent Maryland Cooperative Extension recommendations." This means you will not be able to use the "I did not know" defense if you are caught violating the most recent regulations. It is your responsibility as a business owner to keep yourself up to date on all laws and standards governing your company and its activities, including environmental matters.

Lawn fertilizers

The fertilizers that make lawns green and healthy contain three major elements: nitrogen, phosphorus, and potassium.

Nitrogen gives the lawn a rich green, thick, and sturdy appearance. This is the "N" on the label describing the formula for any given bag or batch of lawn fertilizer. The formula is three numbers, as in 20-10-10. The "20" is the nitrogen. The number varies according to the intensity or strength of the nitrogen content in that batch of fertilizer.

Phosphorus may also be referred to as phosphate. Phosphorus promotes root growth, winter hardiness and helps grass withstand environmental stress. It is the second number in the formula.

Potassium, sometimes called potash, strengthens grass blades so they bounce back from foot traffic. It also helps grass withstand dry spells.

In recent years, some cities and states have placed limitations on the use of phosphorus in lawn fertilizer. When washed into area streams and lakes, phosphorus is said to contribute to algae "bloom" or overgrowth. Taken to an extreme, overgrown algae and waterweeds can cause poor water quality, odors, and fish kill. These are still controversial rulings, so if you live in an area that has endorsed a phosphorus ban, be sure you stay aware of current regulations. Due to the phosphorus controversy, manu-facturers have created new formulation of lawn fertilizer that re-duce or eliminate phosphorus from the mixture. Leaving grass clippings on the lawn instead of raking them up can help main-tain the level of phosphorus without adding more of this chemi-cal through standard lawn fertilizers.

Testing kits are available to evaluate the chemical composition of your landscaping clients' soil. Professional kits are available at **www.gemplers.com** and **www.professionalequipment. com**, among others. You can also take a soil sample to your local county agricultural agency or commercial laboratory for test-ing. The results of the test will give you far a better guidelines to your customers' lawn needs than guessing at the chemical ratio and automatically spreading a standard fertilizer. If you are not knowledgeable about soil chemistry, you may also consult with a fellow landscaper or agricultural agent who is an expert on chemical applications.

It is important that the fertilizer be in a proper balance. Higher numbers in various chemicals or nutrients do not necessarily mean a greener, healthier lawn. High nitrogen, for instance, can "burn" a lawn by overpowering it, making it brown and dead looking. In addition to its potential as a water pollutant, excess phosphorus can cause deficiency of iron and zinc, micronutrients that are necessary for good plant health. Excess potassium is not directly toxic to plants but can bring about a deficiency in magnesium, another important micronutrient.

There is no one "best" fertilizer. That is why it is best to test the soil, and add only the chemicals it requires. There are, however, some features to look for if you choose a standardized blend. You will want a guaranteed analysis of the formula. It will be on the label at the back of the bag or container. Nitrogen is available in slow-release, water insoluble, quick-release, or slowly available. It is available as inorganic or organic. It can be granular or liquid. It may be labeled ammonium nitrate, calcium nitrate, activated sewage sludge, urea, or one of many other terms.

In an established lawn the likelihood of runoff is lessened because of the density of the turf. Even in this instance, a soaking watering immediately after application will improve its penetration. However, care should be taken to avoid spreading chemical fertilizers on hard surfaces such as walkways and driveways because the nutrients can easily spill over into storm drains that lead into streams and rivers. Be especially careful to clean up spillage of these nutrients on hard surfaces. The same caution applies to frozen ground. There is a temptation to do early fertilizing in the spring when the ground is not yet thawed. This increases the risk of water pollution, because any rainfall or snowmelt on still-frozen ground will cause the nutrients to wash into public waterways.

"Organic" fertilizers and pesticides

Concerns about the environment have produced interest in organic fertilizers and pesticides. "Organic" chemicals or fertilizers are those that occur naturally. They are not man-made in a laboratory or produced from petroleum by some complex, artificial means of production. To be effective, an organic fertilizer must contain the same basic nutrients as factory-produced liquid or granular chemical fertilizers: nitrogen, potassium, and phosphorus. Compost can be a source of these nutrients, but it should be analyzed for composition and formula. Be aware that the word "organic" does not mean there are no environmental effects from this type of fertilizer. Nitrogen and phosphorus from farm runoff and organic landscaping can still have a negative impact on streams, rivers, and lakes, so it is important to use these products properly.

"Activated sewage sludge" is one type of material used for organic fertilizers. It is what you think it is, although it has been sanitized in a sewage treatment facility. Some municipalities give it away, others have arrangements with various entities to haul it off, package it, and either sell it or give it away. There are those who feel that this type of fertilizer has an offensive odor. Customers who are sensitive to this may not want it spread all over their yards.

A number of companies specialize in organic lawn and garden products. One of them is called Cockadoodle DOO, a product of Pure Barnyard. The company warns that people who are allergic to corn should avoid the dust of its product, which is produced from animal waste, and there is also a warning that people who are allergic to chickens or feathers should not handle it. As with all products, organic or artificial, read the warning labels, not only for yourself, but also for your customer. Before you spread something around a homeowner's yard, be sure you know if it is safe in general, and acceptable to the people who have hired you to work on their property.

Organic nutrient products also are made from bat guano (high in nitrogen), fish meal (high nitrogen and good phosphorus, little potassium), and kelp meal, which comes from seaweed and contains trace minerals that help grass and plants flourish. Organic fertilizers are typically slow-release products that work through the breakdown of natural nutrients. These are not products that you spread on Saturday and watch the grass turn greener in the following week. They should be spread as part of a season-long plan and given a longer period to work. Pure Barnyard offers commercial-grade products for landscape professionals, as do other producers of organic fertilizers.

If you feel that organic products are good for the environment and want to separate yourself from other landscape professionals, set up and market yourself as an organic landscaper, qualifying and applying for all applicable certifications. You will attract customers who are drawn to organic lifestyle firms. There are significant state and local regulations that legitimize your claim of "organic." Be sure you follow these rules, or define which of your services is organic and which is not.

Learn as much as you can about these products. Take courses at your local college to increase your knowledge and qualifications. Consult with licensed companies about working with you as you increase your knowledge. Do not apply anything to a yard until you and your customer know what it is and what it will do.

Pesticides

Pesticides are the most regulated area of the landscape industry. There are federal, state, and in many cases, local laws governing their use. In fact, there are so many aspects to this type of product that the United States Environmental Protection Agency has a Web site devoted to it: The National Pesticide Information Center, **npic.orst.edu/epareg**.

Pesticides are substances that prevent, destroy, repel, or mitigate anything defined as a pest. The term pesticide is not confined to substances that kill or repel insects, but include mice, moles, chipmunks, weeds (otherwise known as plants you do not want), fungi, bacteria, and viruses. The primary law that governs the use of pesticides is the Federal Insecticide, Fungicide, and Rodenticide Act. It directs the EPA to oversee all types of pesticides. The EPA, in turn, cautions that every state has is own regulations and laws and primary responsibility for enforcing them. Counties, cities, and townships may have their own regulations and enforcement agencies. It can get confusing and technical, so think about whether you want to obtain your own certification and license, or find a licensed service and let them take care of it for you.

Maryland, for example, requires approved training in such things as pesticide safety, biology, control, storage and disposal. A commercial applicator must pass a core examination plus exams on each of the pesticide applications he or she plans to perform. The certificate must be renewed each year. In New York commercial lawn care companies are required to notify customers 48 hours in advance of pesticide applications, cost to the customer, warnings labels of any product being applied, and lawn care signs in the yard for at least 24 hours after the application. State regulations change, some yearly, so it is important to keep informed about the latest chemical regulations in your area.

One successful landscape company in Maryland also services customers in the District of Columbia and Virginia. Laws are different in each of these jurisdictions, increasing the required paperwork to headache level. This company decided to use other, licensed chemical and pesticide firms to handle such things. Pesticide applicators also must obtain special insurance to cover the costs of environmental or health disasters. If applied properly, pesticides can take care of the things you and your customer want removed or prevented, such as weeds and flower-eating bugs. Some of the products are toxic and must be respected and used carefully. Do not perform pesticide application without proper training. This is not only illegal; it could harm you and your customer.

As with fertilizers, there is a growing movement toward environmentally friendly and organic pesticides. The reasons are powerful. Chemicals used improperly can harm the environment and kill or sicken people and wildlife. Pesticides are the number two cause of household poisoning in the United States. Commercial applicators are likely to be more cautious and knowledgeable than a homeowner who purchases a bug spray and dispenses it without bothering to read the label, but the dangers are there for all applicators of strong chemicals.

Researchers around the world are working on organic or "natural" pesticides, with some success. For instance, bacteria called Bt (Bacillus thuringiensis) kills insects that feed on plants. It is a powder that is sprinkled or dusted on the plant you want to protect. Its primary benefit is its human-friendly quality. Unfortunately, it can take days to kill the bugs and will not know a butterfly from a beetle. Bt has been around for a while; only been recently have its applications have been understood and refined. The company Pharm Solutions has several products certified as organic by the U.S. Department of Agriculture, including products to control fungi. Some are oil or soap products similar to the ones that your great grandmother may have used.

As with fertilizers, a label of "organic" does not mean there are no environmental or health risks. An organic product can be toxic. Educate yourself about any product or substance you plan to use and follow directions. Truly organic gardeners tout the benefits of using plants to repel specific insects. Mint, for example, is said to repel ants and aphids. Garlic is reputed to repel certain beetles, and marigolds are credited with repelling whiteflies, tomato hornworms, and thrips. If you choose to define your business as organic you must avoid using non-organic products, including traditional chemical and so-called artificial pesticides. As your business grows and develops, your knowledge and skill will increase, allowing you to better understand your company's place in the market and the products and services you feel comfortable providing.

CASE STUDY: ORGANIC LANDSCAPE & DESIGN CO., ANTHONY VITALE

Organic Landscape & Design Co.
PO Box 184
Madison, NJ 07940
973-593-0268
www.organiclandscapedesign.com

Anthony Vitale, owner of Organic Landscape & Design Co., grew up with plants and gardens favored by his Italian-American family, and worked as a landscaper in high school. After graduating from college with degrees in music and marketing, Vitale did not want an indoor job. "I wanted to keep doing gigs and be my own boss," he says. "I didn't feel there would be a salary cap. I could make as much money as my brain could afford, and if I needed to get away, I could take time off."

Although he was drawn to work outside, Vitale had deep concerns about using chemicals and artificial fertilizers. (His father died young from cancer that might have been triggered by using garden chemicals.) "I was convinced it would be better to do things organically, as far as my health was concerned," he said. "But there was no organic landscaping industry when I started my business in the mid-1980s. Still, there were organic farms in Pennsylvania, which was not far away. So I decided to market my business as an organic alternative to conventional landscape business."

The concept of organic landscaping was a hard sell at first. Vitale worked with companies like Fertrell that usually worked with farmers, not landscapers. He would take soil samples to be tested, and then discussed what products would make the yard flourish. "Calcium is often very deficient in New Jersey soil, and it's actually more important to the growth of the lawn than potassium, phosphorus, or nitrogen," he said. Vitale adds calcitic lime to get the proper pH. When soil is balanced, fertilizer is absorbed more readily by the plant itself, and increased microbial activity beneath the soil's surface impedes fungus growth.

Now it is easier to find organic lawn products from outlets like **www.espoma.com** and **www.convertedorganics.com**, which do not use human fecal material or other unsafe components. Educating the customer is essential, Vitale said. "I am to the landscaping industry what a preventative medicine doctor is to the medical industry."

Today's topsoil is manufactured from clay, compost, and sand, and you do not know where the ingredients came from. "Organics feed the soil and the environment; conventional pesticides and fertilizers treat the plant itself," he said. His methods put more biodiversity into the soil. "It just creates a happy place for plants. Although, using chemically-based stuff judiciously and sparingly can be a safe alternative."

Chapter Twelve

Hiring Outdoor Workers

The day-to-day lawn care business requires people who show up, do the work, and close up shop at night. When your level of commitment to customers reaches a level you alone cannot sustain, it is time to consider hiring an employee, either fulltime or part time, permanent, or temporary. You would do well to use the same high standards for temporary employees that you would for those who you expect to be long-term. Everyone who works for your company represents your company. The competence, friendliness, and courtesy your customers expect should be reflected in every person you hire.

There are two types of workers for your business: those who are key to your business development and growth and those who work part time. The *key worker* is the person you will rely on for day-to-day operations, the man or woman you know will be there for you, who knows your operation, your products and services, and who knows how to deal with customers. This person is more than somebody who knows how to mow a lawn. This is someone you want to keep for the long term. As a general measure, you should pay this person well, offer whatever benefits you can, and keep them happy and on the job. An employee like this is rare and your competitors will be happy to steal him or her from you.

The second type of employee you may consider is temporary-- those who come and go. You add people as the work demands, taking them on for big projects, letting them go when the job is finished. The challenge is to reduce the number of temporary hires who create problems or need extensive training. If you are paying someone to learn how to do a job, only to let that person go, you are training that person to work for someone else, probably a competitor. However, if you are fortunate and choosey, it can work the other way; you can enjoy the benefits of a temporary worker who has been trained by someone else.

Ideally, you will find someone who has knowledge in experience in lawn care, landscaping, and gardening. If you come across that kind of individual, find out why he is not employed. Experience alone is not a good indicator of a satisfactory employee. After all, this person might have been fired because he was not dependable or competent. Successful business managers recommend zero tolerance for any bad behavior, whether it is showing up late, laziness, or constant complaining without getting anything done. Make your policies clear from day one and put them in writing, so there will be no misunderstandings if you fire someone at the job site.

So where do you find employees for your business? It is not unusual for prospective employees to contact businesses looking for work. They may see your truck or notice you at a job site and offer their services. Eager, experienced workers may drop into your lap, especially when the economy is not doing well.

When times are good, you may have to be a little more proactive in your search.

Newspaper or Internet ads are effective. Put one together outlining exactly what you are looking for, outline the work and hours, but consider whether you want to put the hourly pay in the ad. In some areas of the country, help-wanted ads for landscaping companies routinely contain the starting hourly wage. In others, a wage range is listed, and in other places words such as "competitive hourly wage" are used instead of specific numbers. Get to know the pay scales in your area for the work you want done, check the ads being placed by your competitors, and use those standards as guides. Also be sure to state in your ad that applicants must be currently eligible to work in the US for any employer.

This is the only "pre-screening" you can legally do to make sure you are not hiring an ineligible worker. If you live in a large metropolitan area you may get better results from community papers than from the large dailies that cover areas a hundred or more miles. Online services such as CraigsList.com and its local competitors may be a cost effective form of advertising. Just be sure your applicants are local. It is not wise to employ someone who lives two hours away and drives an old car that may or may not start on any given day.

Keep in mind that it is illegal to place an ad that discriminates against anyone because of race, sex, age, religion, and other factors. You are looking for someone who can do the job, no matter what other qualities the person has or does not have. List your telephone number and/or email address in the ad rather than an address or post office box number. If you list your address, and you are working out of your home, you may have unexpected visitors at your door at all hours. Using a post office box will delay response time, so is not desirable for hiring in a rush.

If there is a college in your area that offers training in landscaping or gardening, talk to an administrator or teacher about placing an ad on a bulletin board for students who are looking for jobs in the field. Perhaps the teacher is willing to ask in class if anyone wants or needs a job or internship with a landscaping company. Your networking in professional organizations also can be a source of leads for employees. As you ask around, try to find out why any given worker is available. Some will have been downsized for any number of reasons, others will have been fired. Find out why.

If you do all of the above, you will have many résumés to consider on your desk. Sort through them and eliminate those that do not fit your needs or seem otherwise inappropriate. Rank the remaining résumés by factors such as experience, recommendations from former employers, and other criteria that are important to you. You are searching for best employee you can find; it will pay off in the long term to put some effort into it. You also may find that you have five or six qualified candidates, at least at this stage, before you actually interview anyone. Decide who you want to talk to and arrange personal interviews at your office or, if there is not enough space there, at a local coffee shop.

Interviews

The interview process begins on the telephone, as you are setting a time for a personal meeting. The first thing to consider is the attitude of the person on the other end. Is he or she friendly or surly? Do not confuse an inability to articulate with a bad attitude. Someone may not have much formal education but have experience and a positive attitude that will overcome poor grammar. What is the overall demeanor of the person you are talking to on the telephone? Does this sound like a person you would like to be around? Some people may be shy about admitting they do not have much experience or some other negative. Lack of experience is not as big a drawback as someone whom you suspect is being evasive, trying to pass off work experience at a fast food restaurant as a qualification to work for you as a landscape worker.

Why do they want the job? Do they have an interest in landscaping and gardening, or do they just need some money? Select the most suitable applicants before you schedule face-to-face meetings. You will want to know whether they have experience with the tools and equipment they will be using as your employee.

During the personal interview apply the same standards you would expect your customers to use. How is this person presenting himself or herself? In the real world it is unlikely a landscaping job applicant will arrive for an interview wearing a suit, but is the person clean? Is clothing torn or dirty? Does he or she look you in the eye? If the prospective employee claims to have experience, ask them two or three questions that require some knowledge to answer. You do not have to be challenging or harsh in your questioning. You can be friendly, even funny. You simply want to determine to the best of your ability whether this person is being honest with you. You might want to present a scenario and ask how the applicant would start, perform, and finish the task you describe.

Review the applicant's résumé and ask questions about gaps in work history or lack of recommendations or past employers. A young man whose only experience is cutting mom and dad's lawn may not be a bad prospect as long as he freely admits that that is the only work he has ever done. Someone who tries to turn that work history into a major qualification to work for you might not be as desirable as an employee. If you have the sense that your candidate is lying, be cautious about hiring him or her. It is easier to not hire someone in the first place than to fire him or her after the fact.

Before you interview anyone, read up on rules about discrimination in hiring. Some questions are forbidden. You may not ask about a person's religion, politics, or sexual preference. Your questions should track the qualifications for the job, not outside interests or qualities the prospect has no control over. Someone who is frail and cannot perform manual labor is not right for a job that requires hard, physical work. That same standard would not apply to an office worker whose most challenging physical effort will be moving paper from one side of a desk to another or using the telephone.

It is not out of bounds to ask "what if" questions during a job interview. "What if a customer told you install a sprinkler system that was not part of the work order?" is an appropriate question. "I would advise him or her to contact you," is a good answer. Discuss the job with the applicant, describing in detail what you would want that person to do. Check their reactions. If the candidate responds in a way that is completely unreasonable, smile, thank them for their time and end the interview. Also avoid the applicant whose interview style is to present a list of demands which he or she expects you to meet. Someone who says, "I do not work Mondays and I have to leave by 3 p.m. three days a week, and my bad back means I cannot lift heavy things," and so on, is not a positive prospect. In some cases, though, there can be valid reasons why someone needs to leave work early on certain days. If all other things are acceptable, and you have not found your worker yet, you may decide to hire someone regardless of their special circumstances. However, think it through carefully, because you will be risking legal action if you later try to dismiss this employee because he or she has special requirements.

With each job applicant, try to see the person objectively. Is this someone you want to be around every day? Someone a customer would like and trust? Someone you believe can help your company grow? All of these things matter.

You will be looking for people for the short, medium, and long term. The short term is today and tomorrow and next week, when you have lawns that need to be cut and bushes that need to be trimmed. Someone has to get those jobs done. The medium term is the rest of the season and the extra work that must be planning and completed. The long term is next year and beyond, when your projects expand along with your employees. Today's hire might be tomorrow's foreman. Is he or she up to the job?

Hiring people you can promote is important because it gives employees reassurance that they can grow along with your company and provides incentives for superior performance. Ambition can work for you. Do not be reluctant to hire the smartest people you can find.

Once you have narrowed your list and found the person or persons you would like to hire, check them out. Call former employers to inquire about their work histories and performance. Be aware that many former employers will be reluctant to offer bad news about someone. Know the qualities you want to inquire about and ask specific questions. If you just ask, "What can you tell me about Bob?" you will probably get an answer as general as the question. "He was all right." You want to know if Bob showed up on time, did what he was supposed to do, and caused any problems. Listen for what Bob's former employee is *not* telling you. If his former employer is distant or does not seem as though he has much to say about Bob, this may be a warning sign. On the other hand, if he says, "I would hire him again in a minute," you have the answer you need.

Once you have made a decision, call Bob and give him the good news. Tell him clearly, as you should have done during the interview, that you have a probationary period, 60 or 90 days (longer or shorter as you chose) during which he can quit or you can let him go with no hard feelings and no obligation on either side. Send him a confirmation letter outlining your work policies and what is expected of him. This can be a separate document if you like. Again, as with customers, it is best to have all requirements and expectations in writing.

Contact everyone else you have interviewed and explain that you have made a decision to hire someone else and keep the résumés of people you think might be suitable in the future. Wish everyone well and thank them for their time.

Even after you select a candidate, keep the other appropriate-seeming résumés and contact information. You never know when you may need another employee, and if someone who applied previously happens to be available, you will save yourself time in finding your next hire.

Some communities restrict how many employees a home-based business can have. Check your local zoning and other regulations before you commit to a number of people parking their cars, servicing your trucks, and doing other business-related activities in the neighborhood. If you face such restrictions you will be forced to either rent business space or arrange to meet all of your workers at job sites or other locations.

New Employee Paperwork

No matter whom you hire, you will have to fill out and send in or retain certain government documents. These include W-4 forms, the Employee's Withholding Allowance Certificate, and the W-5, for employees with a child, if they qualify for advance payment of earned income credit. Check the IRS site or **http://business. gov/business-law/forms/** to download forms.

Immigration Concerns

In addition to the W-4 and W-5, you and your employee are required by federal law to file form I-9, Employment Eligibility Verification, within the first three days of employment. Employees fill out Section I on their first day of employment. If the employment will last less than 3 days, the employer must verify work authorization and fill out Section 2 the first day, as well. This requirement applies to everyone—US citizens, permanent residents, and temporary or long-term foreign workers. You may not use form I-9 as a way to screen prospective employees, however. That is considered discrimination. You bring out the form for verification *after* the person is hired. Certain documents are necessary to provide proof, such as a US driver's license or passport, or a permanent resident (green) card. However, there are many different combinations of documents that provide acceptable proof of eligibility to work in the US. Check out the US Citizenship and Immigration (USCIS) site for more information on requirements and how to verify: **www.uscis.gov/files/article/E3eng.pdf** According to USCIS, an employer is not required to know with absolute certainty whether a document submitted by an employee is genuine or false. However, the employer must examine the actual document, not a photocopy (although a certified copy of a birth certificate is acceptable), and make a good faith determination that the document appears to relate to the employee, appears to be genuine, and is included on the list of Acceptable Documents for Form I-9.

The I-9 forms are retained by the employer, and made available for inspection by appropriate authorities, for three years after the date of hire, or one year following the end of employment – whichever date is *later*. For long-term employees, it is a good idea to have written policies for re-verification before the I-9 expires, and for persons whose documents are currently in process by the Immigration and Naturalization Service (INS).

Also note that you cannot restrict employment to those with a particular citizenship or immigration status. There are different immigration categories of people who are authorized to work in the United States. You do not want to violate federal anti-discrimination laws.

At the same time, you do not want to hire those not eligible to work in the U.S. There are penalties for employing illegal immigrants that can have a strong negative impact on your business financially and in your customer relationships. As with all other areas of your business management, do what you must to remain within the law.

Some professional landscape associations, such as the California Landscape Contractors' Association (CLAC) and the Associated Landscape Contractors of Colorado (ALCC) post regular informative bulletins about immigration and undocumented workers' concerns on their websites. While often thought of as primarily targeting migrant farm workers who are picking or planting crops, H-2B temporary agricultural labor visas are a common immigration status for landscape workers as well. New rules will take effect in 2010 for workers under this designation. The announcement was made in December 2008 at **www.uscis.gov/ files/article/H-2B_18dec2008.pdf**

Various pieces of legislation have recently been introduced to counter widespread unemployment of US citizens in 2009, so check the USCIS site regularly for current information: **www.uscis.gov**

If you need a good reason to join a professional landscape, lawn care, or nursery organization, the fact that all of these groups have lobbyists in Washington, and communicate the pros and cons of legislation that will affect your business is something to keep in mind.

Drug Testing

State laws vary as to the benefits or regulations of drug testing for job applicants and current employees. It may be more advantageous as an employer to limit drug testing to job applicants, rather than current employees. Employers generally are permitted to require that applicants for their company be "drug free", and since the person is not yet an employee, the testing is unlikely to erode company morale.

Applicant drug tests can be circumvented, of course, but advance testing puts the potential employee on notice that your company does not approve drug use and may test in the future, at random (although such tests must be conducted within legal guidelines.)

The US Chamber of Commerce website offers detailed information about drug testing, as well as a state-by-state interactive map that you can click to see what drug testing policies are applicable to your own state. It is available at **http://business.uschamber. com/P05/P05_1075.asp**

Another useful online source of information is the Labor and Employment Law Blog at **www.laborandemploymentlawblog. com/2008/07/drug-testing-jo.html**

Training

Training your first new employee can seem to be an intimidating, time-consuming task, but think of it as a way to nurture a long-term relationship and build trust and cooperation with a person who will eventually be a great help to your business.

Imagine that you have hired Bob as your first full-time employee. You cannot just drop him off at a customer's house and instruct him to cut the grass. It is important that everyone you hire be trained in your company policies, equipment, maintenance, customer satisfaction requirements, appearance, and all of the other qualities that make your business.

Start off by preparing yourself with a written task list, where you describe each job in detail. These job descriptions can be refined as time goes on, and can eventually be collected together to provide a handy guide booklet for all new employees. If you are a better speaker than a writer, you can record a description of the tasks onto a tape or digital recording. You can even describe a job while you are doing it. Later, this recording can be transcribed and edited for your employee booklet.

Prioritize the tasks you want your employee to perform, so when you start training, you begin with the simplest or most important task first. No one can be expected to learn everything at once, so break down the jobs into chunks that are easy to understand. Handout sheets can help reinforce what it is you want to get done. If your employee does not read well, or speak English well, you may want to use drawings on your handouts to help get the points across.

Show him or her the equipment and how it works. He or she should know how to fuel mowers, blowers, hedge trimmers or other tools. Your new employee should know what every tool is for, preferably by hands-on demonstration and working together on a job, at least once. It is better if you can share the work at the same job sites for several days, especially with the first employee.

This will help create an atmosphere of teamwork and cooperation, which is vitally important for a constructive work environment. It will also help you understand your new employee, see
him or her in action, and give you the opportunity to make gentle
corrections if some part of a task is not performed the way you
want it to be done.

As you instruct new employees about equipment, stress safety.
Mowers, chain saws, and other lawn and garden items can cause
serious injury. Use eye protection and possibly ear protection
as well. If you will be digging, show him or her the appropriate
measures to take to avoid digging into cable or gas lines. Instruct
all employees on how to avoid back injuries, and how to maintain a safe job site for themselves and the customer's family. Injuries on the job may happen from time to time, but you can avoid
major mishaps through proper safety instruction. Many states
have specific safety requirements for your businesses, and special training procedures that are required on a regular schedule,
so this is another area where it pays to know the local laws.

Never stop training. You, as the owner, have an obligation to yourself and your business to improve your knowledge and skills. You
will want to pass that determination to stay on the leading edge
of your business down to those who work for you. Bob may one
day be your foreman. What he learns from you about the values
of your company will be transferred to everyone who works for
you. If you are sloppy, Bob will be sloppy, and so will everybody
else. Lead by example and maintain high standards of safety,
training, and customer service.

Set goals for the company, yourself, and your new employee. At some point he or she will be working alone, without you to supervise everything he or she does. Make it clear from the outset that you will always go to completed job sites to make sure everything is as it should be. Your employee should have no problem with that. This does not mean you must examine every blade of grass or tree branch, but it ensures that the owner will be around to see that the lawn was actually cut, the driveway and sidewalk edged, and the mulch spread to the proper depth. This accomplishes two things: your employees know you are aware of what is going on, and the customer will see that you supervise the project or contract they have hired you for. Paying close attention to new employees also helps ward off surprise, such as angry telephone calls from customers who want to know why somebody "weeded" their garden by pulling out all the flowers.

Offer to help your employees obtain certification in a number of landscaping areas by providing financial assistance or incentives. Invest in videos, books, manuals, and other material that can help improve skills and knowledge. Trade associations and professional groups will be a good source of this material, as will local educational institutions and online resources.

Ask your employees about their career dreams and goals and help them achieve them. You will grow as they grow. Eventually, one or more of your employees may outgrow your company and move on to start new businesses. If that is the case, wish them well. It is a sign of your own confidence to show by example that growth and knowledge are good. Never be afraid to help someone become better.

If you are wise in your hiring decisions, the people who work for you are making money for you. Some employers treat laborers badly, seeing them as expendable, but they make money for their employers and they should be treated with respect. The cost of your employees is factored into the prices your customers pay, so they do not cost you anything. The customer pays their salaries and benefits; it is in your interest to be encouraging and helpful, even as you demand the best effort from your workers.

How do you do this? Money is the primary motivator. If you cannot afford to offer someone a raise, give him or her a bonus for a job well done. If you have a large project that is completed on time and you are making a handsome profit, share the wealth by adding something to your employee's paycheck with a thank-you note. If Bob has been working hard and long hours, give him a day off with pay when the pace slows down a little. The best bosses manage people with praise, not criticism. A note of thanks, a pat on the back, can go a long way to create a positive, cooperative work environment where each person feels supported and contributes for the good of all. Treat your employees with respect, maintain high standards, and reward performance. The workers who cannot or will not meet these standards will fall by the wayside, either by quitting or being let go.

Payroll and Benefits

While you are doing research for competitive pricing, you may also want to research pay rates for outdoor workers in your area. If you are expecting to hire only general labor for yard work, you may be able to pay the minimum wage and still satisfy the employee. But paying slightly above that wage may be worth it to ensure reliable, effective workers.

National average wage rates are available through the government business surveys, online at **www.bls.gov/bls/blswage.htm**. Data is searchable by both area and occupation.

Benefits are another incentive to keep good workers. It is so difficult these days for workers to find jobs with benefits that you may attract and keep the best workers around. Health insurance, life insurance, and vacation pay are always welcomed, and today, these benefits are not taken for granted. However, they are expensive to offer, so you will need to build in sufficiently high customer rates and have enough customers to pay the bills. If you are looking for a benefit package to offer your employees, check with a small business insurance broker or see if your local chamber of commerce has special insurance programs for small businesses.

Subcontracting and Partnering/Referral

Subcontractors

Subcontractors make sense for one-time projects or for tasks that you cannot or do not want to perform, such as chemical applications and testing. Also, if you have a contract to redo an entire yard, complete with gardens, pathways, and stone walls, you may not have the expertise or time to actually construct stone walls and walkways, so you would look for someone who can do the job at a price you feel is fair to you and the customer. If you have done your networking in professional organizations you will know who the best people are in your region. Maintaining a list of contractors and their skills and specialties can be an important and profitable way to expand your business and add to your portfolio.

If you choose to use subcontractors, remember that whoever they are and whatever they do, they represent you and your company. The customer may not know or care that the people who show up to build the stone wall or cut down a tree do not work for you, but they will care about the quality of the job. Be sure to screen your subcontractors by doing background checks on the quality of their work and explain your standards to them. Also, check to make sure they have their own liability and workers' compensation insurance policies because yours will not cover them.

Specialty subcontractors can save you money and time on tasks like chemical applications. They will have the permits and equipment you have not yet acquired, for lawn seeding with water (hydro), tree planting, trimming and removal, and designing or installing features of landscape architecture such as patios and walkways.

If you are not licensed to apply chemicals, for example, you will probably want to be prepared early in your start-up phase to partner with a licensed contractor who can provide this service. By networking within the profession, you will be able to search out the most competent providers in your geographical area. Introduce yourself to the owners *before* you need their help. Explain your situation, that you are actively marketing your particular services, but will need some assistance for chemical applications. Your potential subcontractor will probably be glad to hear about your business needs, because every job you bring in is one that he or she does not have to find.

At this point—well before you have a chemical applications requirement in hand—you can start ironing out the facts and figures of how you and your future subcontractor will come to terms. Discuss pricing, how far in advance they need to be contacted, what sort of terms they require for payment, and any other special needs. You do not need to identify a particular customer in advance. There is no reason to undercut your ability to sell the job by simply handing the project over to the chemical-applications specialist. Instead, get a figure from him on what he will charge you for the work. Ask for estimates if you bring him just a single job, or several bids. Also ask if there would be any discount if he became your exclusive supplier of chemical services. Serious talks should lead to a written agreement that both of you can live with. Discuss price with the supplier only, and avoid disclosing what you think the customer will pay.

Conversations about what the customer pays should remain between partners in your business, not between primary and subcontractors. Always mark up a subcontractor's price. Ten percent is not unreasonable; you may even increase the margin. You have a business to run and issues with subcontractors can become complex. You must take the initiative to locate and set up an agreement with the subcontractor. Also, you will ultimately be responsible for his or her performance.

If you hire a subcontractor to build a retaining wall and he does an inadequate job, the customer will call you, not him. If your name is on the contract, you are the one who must stand behind the entire job. Most customers will not be sympathetic to the explanation, "My subcontractor messed up." The customer is likely to respond by saying, "That is not my problem. Make it right."

In some cases, you may prefer to not be an intermediary in the service provided. For example, if you refer a customer to a specialized tree removal service, which you cannot perform, you may choose to advise them to work out their own deal. In such a case, whatever does or does not happen is not your direct responsibility. Sometimes, if you send one of your customers directly to a specified company with a recommendation, that company will pay you a "finder's fee" for the referral, but you cannot count on this unless you and the specialized service provider have worked out an agreement. Be sure you give out names of only reputable firms. Anyone you recommend to a customer will, in the customer's mind, be a representative of you. If the job is not completed in a satisfactory way, the customer will judge *you* because you recommended a company that delivered poor-quality service. This is a risk you should take seriously.

In business, as in life, relationships matter. Professional relationships tend to be grouped around similar standards. If your accountant has high standards, chances are good that a lawyer he recommends will have similar standards. You must strive for the same level of performance that you would demand in someone else. Thus, you can be confidant that not only is your performance high, but also the performance of anyone else you do business with, either as a subcontractor or a referral. Ultimately, this level of excellence will serve you well with referrals and the people you do business. Make clear to anyone you are considering as a subcontractor what you expect in terms of service and quality.

Consider hiring subcontractors for one-time projects or special products or services such as chemical applications, masonry, re-grading yards, and other jobs for which you neither have the training nor equipment. Mark up the subcontractor's price to provide yourself a profit. No matter how the job turns out, you will be the one the customer turns to, and if there are problems, you must have a way to financially deal with it. Be sure to write down every detail of the job in both your contract and your written bid.

Developing Mutual Referral Relationships

Just as you will want to locate people to help you with the chores you do not want to perform, there may be ample opportunity for you to be referred to a customer by someone else. How do you establish mutual referral relationships?

To start with, it is essential to provide top quality work. No one will knowingly recommend a supplier or service that is careless or sloppy. As you start your business and demonstrate your commitment to excellence, the word will get around among other professionals in your community. You and the work you perform will be judged by other businesses, just as you are already evaluating others. This is positive for you, as long as you are giving your best effort at every opportunity. If you become known for providing top-of-the-line service, you will begin getting recommendations from other professionals who are not direct competitors. It never hurts to "ask for the sale," that is, to ask your fellow professionals to steer business your way. You may even wish to set up a "finder's fee" arrangement with some of them.

As soon as you obtain your business license and a tax number, you can approach growers and other wholesale outlets to establish accounts and relationships. Explain who you are and ask what they supply and what type of relationship they are open to.

It may be that some of them will not want to deal with a small, new company. Others will welcome the business and be happy to work with you. Be aware that you will not get the pricing of larger, more-established companies that are competing with you, but you should be able to negotiate prices that you can mark up while still being competitive.

Product or Service Licensing, Joint Ventures, Dealerships

Landscapers, lawn service companies, and nurseries may all benefit from some of the special categories of business operations such as licensing of products or services, joint ventures, and dealership operations. None of these categories are likely avenues for startup profits, but once your business is underway they may be worthwhile. Research some of the possibilities early to see where your business might fit in later on.

Partnerships are ongoing arrangements between two companies or entities, that agree to share profits and losses. A joint venture is the establishment by two separate entities or companies of a third entity that joins together for the completion of a particular project. In this third, "joint," entity, the two founding companies agree to share their profits and losses. The joint venture will terminate when the project is completed. Partnerships, however, continue to share their profits and losses indefinitely. They do not require the formation of a separate entity for each project they perform together.

An example of a joint venture could occur if a landscape design company joined forces with a nursery to bid on a major contract to design landscaping and provide plantings for a major subdivision or a public park. The joint venture would have its own name, tax status, accounting, and would operate as a separate company for the entire length of time that the project was underway. At the end of that period, the joint venture would dissolve.

Although there are several legal licenses that are applicable to the outdoor services industry, such as special contractor licenses and chemical applications licenses, the type of licensing we are referring to is what you pay for or offer for sale to others. For example, if you personally develop a special software product for your landscape business that is especially simple to use, you may want to offer a software license to other landscapers so they can use the software too. Or you may pay a fee and purchase a license to use a particular software product yourself, or you may negotiate a licensing fee to be the sole landscaper in your area to offer a particular type of branded compost enhancer. See more about licenses here: **www.tenonline.org/art/0402.html**

A dealership is essentially a franchise arrangement or license with a product manufacturer to sell a product to the public with a markup over its wholesale price. Dealerships may have geographic exclusivity, so the designated dealer is the only outlet in a particular area permitted to distribute this product. Obtaining a dealership usually involves a substantial investment, but you may decide that the value of a particular trademark brings credibility to your business. Be sure to engage your attorney and accountant to help you evaluate any franchises that you may be considering. An impulse buy is not in your best interest. If you are serious about offering a particular product or service through a dealership or distributorship arrangement, try to locate a dealer — not one referred by the manufacturer — in a distant area. Tell them you are considering this venture and ask what their experience has been.

Additional Schooling

Whether you attend workshops, college courses, or conferences, keeping yourself and your staff in a state of constant learning is most helpful in building a successful enterprise. Many colleges and universities, as well as state or local field extension services, conduct courses on horticulture, safe application of chemicals, construction basics, maintaining fish or lily ponds, and dozens of other programs that will broaden your knowledge base and possibly open doors to new services or techniques that will help you acquire better skills and become more prosperous. Getting your credentials, and credentialing your staff members in a field related to horticulture is bound to improve your credibility with customers. At the same time, a foundation in plant sciences will serve you well throughout your career, since you will have a better understanding of the underlying concepts in plant care.

In some cases you may also benefit by training on the job under an experienced landscaper or patio construction supervisor. There is no substitute for hands-on experience. Working for a successful lawn care, landscaping firm, or nursery can be considered in depth schooling. Keep your eyes and ears open on the job. You will learn how to find good suppliers, how to negotiate relationships, how to talk with customers, how to quote jobs.

CASE STUDY: GARDEN OF EVA LANDSCAPE DESIGN CREW, EVA KNOPPEL

Garden of Eva Landscape Design Crew
743 Hudson Avenue
Los Angeles, CA 90038
323-285-5027

Eva Knoppel is a licensed landscape contractor with a degree in molecular biology. In the mid-90s, she gave up the world of science to start a plant nursery, which led to the landscape design business. She sold the nursery when the demands of the landscaping business became too great to maintain both businesses. Today, she designs and installs hardscaping — patios and other hard surfaces — and water elements such as fountains in middle and upper income homes in southern California.

Knoppel has had as many as 20 employees, but at this time only has 4 full-time people on her payroll. Her staffing is dictated by the scope of the projects she is working on. She provides safety training to everyone who works for her and seeks out employees who have knowledge of landscape design and installation.

She does not provide weekly lawn maintenance, explaining that the Los Angeles area is saturated with companies and individuals who cut grass for low prices, making it difficult for a full-service company to make a profit cutting lawns. Instead, she offers specialty maintenance on the plants that are part of her landscape designs.

Knoppel works with both residential and commercial customers, but prefers residential business. Her prices are middle-to-upper level, always allowing for a reasonable margin to maintain the financial health of her business. She does no commercial application of chemicals.

She works with architects to bring balance and beauty to the landscapes and yards, surrounding their projects and helps them understanding the proper placement of shrubs, trees, and flowers. Knoppel does no marketing beyond maintaining an Internet presence. The bulk of her business comes from word-of-mouth, proving once again that a long list of satisfied customers is the best form of marketing.

SECTION SIX
Your Customers

Chapter Thirteen

Finding Customers—or Helping Them Find You

When you planned your business, you already decided what kind of target customer is most likely to be interested in the services you provide. So how do you let these people know you have opened your doors? There are dozens of ways to do this. You may want to try them all to see which works best for you. The good news is that it does not have to cost you a lot of money to do this. You do not have to be a large company to engage in effective marketing. Take a look at the following list, and pick a few to start.

Inexpensive Marketing Methods

Business cards

You must have business cards. A simple, clear design with your logo, name, phone number and website is adequate. Hand them out everywhere. Pin them up on bulletin boards. Have them handy whenever you are in a public place, at a trade show, in the home improvement store, or wherever people gather. Prepare your elevator speech (a 30-second rapid fire description of what your business does) and be ready to deliver that speech, with a card, at every opportunity. The more people know who you are and what you do, the more business you will get.

Fliers

Fliers are one-page descriptions of who you are and what you offer. Think of a flier as an enlarged business card. You can make your own flier with word processing software or you can go to a professional printing company and have them design and print fliers for you. Do not use fancy fonts or too many busy items that clutter it up.

Here is a simple example:

Lance's Lawn Care

Quality Lawn Care Services
at Reasonable Prices

MOWING

EDGING

PRUNING

LANDSCAPE DESIGN

SPECIALIZED SERVICES

CALL 555 555 5555

For a no-obligation appointment and price quote

Include all your contact information, but on an 8-1/2 by 11" sheet of paper (or one half that size) you can also make a bulleted list of services (mowing, mulching, trimming, planting, etc.) and add a come-on headline or special deal, if you like. Fliers can be folded in thirds, fastened with a sticker and mailed, or simply carry a stack with you as you drive through the neighborhood where you would like to have more customers. Do not put fliers in the mailbox— that is illegal. Instead, tuck them under windshield wipers or post them on approved message boards around town. Make sure it will not be blown by the wind all over the neighborhood. Fliers scattered over the ground would make a poor introduction for your business.

Web site

You already know the value of the Internet. Links throughout this book demonstrate that it is a valuable resource of business information and contacts. Whether you are searching for federal, state, and local regulations for the use of chemicals, professional organizations, local horticultural classes, information about tree pruning, or any other topic, the Internet is the resource of choice in today's world.

If you have a well designed, search-engine friendly Web site, you will likely attract many new customers through the Internet. Think of your site as an online brochure. In addition to presenting your contact information, you can list all your services, display photographs of your projects, offer special prices for products and services, and post a series of informative bulletins about the care and maintenance of plant life, lawns, and trees.

You will need to find a hosting internet service provider (ISP) where your domain name, such as lanceslawncare.com, will reside. Prices for hosting range from free to $50 per month or more. Many Internet companies specialize in hosting small business Web sites. Chose one that has a good chance of being in business a year or two from now to avoid the hassle of looking for cyberspace because your provider went under.

Web site content

It is possible to spend a small fortune on your Web site design, but a complicated "all the bells and whistles" kind of site is not necessary or even desirable. As a small business owner serving a specific geographic area, you simply need a presence to inform potential customers about your services and products. Keep it simple, clear, and easy to use. A typical landscaping company Web site will have sections or pages with titles like Home Page, Services, Contact Us, and possibly a map showing the company's location, if the business is in a public place and offers access to customers.

Your company name and logo should be displayed prominently on every Web page. Your home page should contain concise statements about your company. It might include your company history and employee background, what you do, your pledge of quality and customer satisfaction, and other information that a potential customer would need to contact you. Keep your mind focused on the customer when you are writing or reviewing the copy for your Web site. State what you can do for *them*.

Keywords are the words and phrases that search engines pick up when a would-be customer types in "lawn mowing" or "tree trimming." If you do not have these words in the content of your Web site, the search engine will not identify you as having those services, and the potential customer will be looking at a list of other landscaping firms. It is important that you list every service you provide in as many ways as possible to ensure that your business is identified by search engines as offering those services. There are numerous references on the Internet that can guide you to the current, correct use of Keywords. Search engine methods are always changing, so stay aware of new trends in searching.

Pictures are effective in conveying the quality of your work. Post them on your Web site as examples of your projects. Before and after shots are particularly useful because the potential customer can see how you and your company can transform a yard from something plain into something beautiful.

Older, established small landscaping companies may no have a Web presence; that is good for you. Either the proprietors are not aware of how much business travels through the Web, or have a level of business they are comfortable with and have no desire to add more customers. You, as a new business owner, may find that strange and self-defeating, but more than one owner of a successful landscaping business states that more business does not necessarily led to more profits. Business growth must be carefully planned to account for cash flow, future expenses, and all of the other elements that accompany growth. Some landscapers are happy with their 20 or 30 customers, who pay them every month, year after year. These competitors may not have a presence on the Web.

If you search for the Web sites of landscaping companies, the list will be in the thousands. Look over as many as you can, asking yourself what you like and dislike about them. Some will be elaborate, some plain. Assume that the elaborate sites represent successful businesses that can afford such a Web presence, because the costs can be substantial for top-of-the-line Web sites.

The primary purpose of your spot on the information superhighway is to bring in customers. To start, you will probably not be selling anything over the Internet. As you examine other Web sites, note the ones that leave you staring at the screen, wondering what you should do next. If you wanted to call that company right now, is there a phone number in front of you, or to you have to go looking for it? If you were a customer in need of a tree service, are you in the right place? Do they have any special prices or services? Learn from the mistakes of others, and, without copying, use what you find appealing about these sites as inspiration for your site.

Web site links

As you spread word of your business through professional associations, vendor contacts, and the other professionals you meet, consider partnerships that go beyond handing out each other's business cards. Internet links are valuable aids for businesses. You can link – and be linked – to your suppliers and professional organizations. Chambers' of commerce often list members on their Web sites, as so other groups. Vendors, the companies with whom you do business, may be willing to link your Web site to theirs. You, in turn, can return the favor with other companies and organizations. Think of it as a form of referral.

With the prevalence of Internet search as a marketing tool, numerous entrepreneurs have set up web addresses list different industries in local areas. You will undoubtedly find your company placed automatically on several of these lists. Sometimes they request a "business review" of the company. While it is unlikely that you can post a favorable review of your business, it cannot hurt to ask a friend or relative to mention your company name in a positive light. Paying a considerable amount of money to these sites is something to consider only on a case-by-case basis. Often, having your own Web site in place is enough.

E-mail newsletter or blog

By acquiring the e-mail addresses of your customers and potential customers, you can create ongoing marketing programs that let them know about special services, seasonal tips, and other helpful information while getting your name out as an expert. Blogging, or regular posts about landscaping, lawn care, or nursery topics is another way to build a strong customer base and improve referrals. Some bloggers have targeted other landscapers as their market. See **www.gopherforum.com** for an example of this activity.

Postcards

Postcards are an inexpensive form of direct mail. Print them up at home on your own printer, or go to a quick-print shop. Include your logo, contact information, and basic services. You can use them in place of flyers or posters — stick them in screen doors, put a few around in the coffee shop, post on neighborhood bulletin boards, etc. You can also mail them, and postcards are cheaper to mail than letters. Use colorful paper to make them noticeable.

Displays at community events

If you have aspirations beyond mowing the lawn, purchasing a table at a community event or home show may be worth the cost. To know if it will pay off, consider what you may lose in time and money if no customer, or just one or two, result from your effort. Estimate how many people will be attending, and whether they will be paying attention to landscapers, lawn care, or nurseries at this event. Offer a special prize — a plant, or a free weeding — in a drawing that may entice people to give you their contact information, including e-mail address. Even if you do not expect to gain immediate customers, sometimes the investment is worth it to gain visibility.

Donate volunteer hours

By offering your services for free for an hour a month to a nature center, public gardens, or park board, you can broaden your network and perhaps make contacts with individuals who can help your business grow. At the same time, you can take pride and satisfaction in the community service you provide.

Door knocking

The easiest way to get customers at first is to go to them directly by knocking on the door, and passing out your business cards and flyers. Introduce yourself to anyone who will shake hands with you, and begin to make appointments. Set aside a few hours every week to canvass for customers. When your Yellow Page ad is not out yet, and your Web site is under development, the only fast way to get customers is to meet prospects and tell them you are in business.

If you do not know what to say, write yourself a little speech on a three-by-five card and read it between houses. Say something like this when you knock on a door:

"Hello. I am from (your business) and I am in the neighborhood offering free estimates on lawn and garden services." Then hand them your flyer, and *smile*. "I would be happy to offer a free, no-obligation consultation for your yard and garden." At this point, some people will close the door without saying anything. Let them go and do not take it personally. Perhaps you would do the same thing if someone came to your door and handed you a flyer. The homeowner may call at a later date. Move on the next house.

Canvass neighborhoods where you think your potential customers live. Upper-income neighborhoods are most frequently targeted because people with money can pay to have someone else take care of their yards. One owner of a landscaping company said, "We provide lawn services to high-end homeowners. We have 100 rich people who pay us a lot of money to take care of their yards." There is a good chance your *potential* customers already have someone doing their lawns, but they could be unhappy with those services and therefore ready to hear what you have to say.

Warning: Some neighborhoods may have "No Soliciting" signs. Heed them. It means you cannot knock on doors, but you might be able to leave a flyer in the door. Check with the homeowner's association for that neighborhood. Closed or gated communities will probably keep you out.

If you have an interested party at the door, the next important step is to *listen*. When potential customers describe problems they are having with their current lawn care company, they are telling you what it will take to get their business. If they are unhappy because the person who currently cuts their grass is often late or does not edge the driveway the customer is ready to abandon the company he or she is using because of this problem. You can learn valuable lessons by watching how and why homeowners or commercial customers keep or fire their landscape companies.

Press releases

You can write up a simple press or news release for area newspapers and radio stations, announcing the opening of your business. Any time you add services or new employees, you can do this again. Often business sections of newspapers will present lists of new businesses. Every mention of your new business opens up another opportunity to gain customers. A simple how-to is available here: **www.wikihow.com/Write-a-Press-Release**.

Direct mail

This is a form of targeted marketing. It works best when the people receiving it are potential customers, not everyone in any given Zip Code. Unfortunately, many direct-mail companies send only by Zip Code or geographic area, not by service category, so a lot of people who receive your material will throw it away. You probably know most of the major players because you have received their material. Money Mailer and ValPak are two of the best known, but there are others. They charge by the volume being mailed and your price will be quoted "per thousand". Let us say the cost is $27 per thousand. If you send out 10,000 of your pieces in any given mailing, it will cost you $270. Most direct mail companies will want you to commit to a six or twelve-month contract. The downside is you cannot pick your exact marketing area. Instead, you chose a zip code or two and that is the area you will be marketing to.

In a general mailing, a homeowner or other recipient will either open the envelope or throw it out. If he or she opens it, it is common to stand over the kitchen trash can, scan the coupons, throw out most of them and keep one or two for a future phone call. Response of 1 percent for any given coupon is good. The response rate will go down if there are five landscaping companies offering coupons in the same mailing, so some direct mail firms will offer exclusivity, but at an extra cost. Chances are that your coupon will be sent in a thick packet of coupons for oil changes, windows, pizza, roofs, and all manner of other products. As you track your leads and what they cost, determine how much business you get from any given form of marketing and what it costs per lead. If you spend $270 on a mailing and get only $100 in business, the cost-per-lead ratio is too low.

An alternative is targeted mailing, which sends material to a select list of potential customers, say homeowners with incomes of $100,000 or higher. Obviously, you want these people to know who you are. Some direct mail firms maintain specialized mailing lists and can tailor your marketing. You will not get a cheap per-thousand rate for these lists. They cost more to put together, they tend to corral a higher response rate, and you send only to people who are potential customers and who have the money to pay for your services. Your dollar output will be higher but if you spend $1,000 for $10,000 worth of business, it is a great investment.

There are variations on these themes. Marketing and mailing firms all have stories to tell you about what a great service they provide. You are ultimately the decision maker about your own marketing and will either benefit or lose from what these firms provide. In terms of your advertising and marketing, there are two basic categories: call-to-action and top-of-mind.

Call-to-action marketing urges the customer to do something "right now," as in, "Call today and receive an additional ten percent off all fall flowers," or "Call today for a free consultation and receive ten percent off the first month's lawn maintenance." You have no doubt seen these ads before. The concept is to get the customer to take some action by offering an incentive. This is designed to get business right now, something you need immediately after you open for business to get money in the door.

Top-of-mind is marketing that brings in business tomorrow, not today. Top-of-mind marketing is getting your name out there and keeping it there, so potential customers will think of you whenever they decide they need your services. Running the same newspaper ad week after week is top-of-mind marketing, even though you might run a coupon now and then, crossing one tactic into another. Passing out business cards every week or month to the same people at professional organizations qualifies as top-of-mind advertising. Your goal is to reach a point where anyone who thinks of landscaping thinks of you. Billboards qualify, as well, because most of them do not try to get you to make a call right now; they want to keep the business name up there as you drive by everyday.

Recognize the difference between the two tactics to avoid dashed expectations. Running a generic "Think of us when you think of landscaping" ad may actually bring in customers, but running one that says, "Act now and save money" may get you better results.

Posters

A poster is usually 11" x 17" or bigger, and describes your service, especially if there is a special deal or sale underway. Posters are usually printed or lettered on heavy card stock. This is often what you use at a community display to let people know who you are and what you provide. Posters can be colorful, and should be well designed to attract attention without confusing the onlooker. Obviously, your phone number and/or Web site address should be prominently displayed. Inexpensive stand-up easels are available at office supply stores if you want to place a poster at reading view on a table.

Truck signage

Put a sign on your truck and on other equipment if it makes sense. You will want people to recognize your company name and logo. A magnetic sign will be cheaper, but a well-executed professional lettering job or decal may be better.

Shirts with logo

Consider investing in company shirts with your company identity prominently displayed. T-shirts are fine for your crew, but something with a collar is best for the owner. You want to present a competent, professional image. If you are going to work and canvassing or networking on the same day, bring a change of clothing and some wipes to clean yourself. Always keep a spare shirt in your vehicle. First impressions are critical and you and your company will be judged in an instant.

Conducting Appointments

Marketing as a tool to bring in leads is only a part of the strategy to grow your business. Another key part is what you do with the leads you get. If you do not get the business, they are not worth much. Getting the appointment is merely an introduction, not a sale. The rest is how you present yourself and the services you offer.

Let us go through a sales call. You are clean, sharp, and wearing a new company shirt with your logo and company name displayed. You have your briefcase, which contains business cards, estimate forms, and maybe some photographs from other jobs. Your appearance and demeanor are part of your marketing and the customer is making mental notes about you and will likely pass these thoughts onto his neighbors, one way or the other.

You introduce yourself and ask, "What can I do for you?" You do not want to introduce yourself and immediately launch into a sales pitch, because you want the customer to tell you what he or she wants. If you launch into a sales pitch about lawn services but the customer wants some bushes trimmed, you may lose the sale. Find out what the customer wants and explain the benefits of using your business. Listen carefully to what the customer says. If they have complaints about the landscaping people they have used in the past, take that information as a clue to making this customer happy enough to not only sign a maintenance contract, but also refer you to their neighbors. You probably will have to answer questions about the size of your business. In your case, size is a benefit. They are dealing directly with the owner and you will personally guarantee quality and timely service. Explain that your standards are high. Keep this in mind as you grow and hire employees. Keep your standards up.

Do not be afraid to ask for the customer's business. Explain what you are offering, assure the homeowner that you will do a good job, and ask for his or her business. Something on the order of, "I would like your business" will do. "Would you like a three-month or a six-month maintenance contract?" also is good, but it must be said with a friendly demeanor that does not convey arrogance. You want to appear confident without seeming pushy. The best marketing is customer satisfaction. Do what you say you will do, when you say you will do it. Listen to what customers say about your services. They will be your best business advisors because they are reacting to the services and products you are selling. If they do not like something, make it right. Keep expectations within reason and deliver more than you promise if you can. It is always better to leave customers thinking you have over-delivered rather than under-delivered.

Cross-selling Your Services

An existing customer is your best asset. It is cheaper and easier to get an existing customer to purchase more of your products and services than it is to find a new customer for those same services and products. What if you have a customer who is paying only for lawn maintenance, but whose yard is ripe for improvement? There is no cost per lead here. This customer already knows you and understands that you show up on time, do a good job, clean up your mess, and listen to her or his needs and concerns. This person is likely to be open to your ideas. The opportunity for you to suggest landscaping improvements is there for you to take.

Your customer list is a valuable marketing opportunity, one your competitors would love to have. If your customer service is good, and you provide quality products and keep your customers happy, you have a great chance of keeping them as clients. Better yet, you have a good chance of getting them to purchase more of what you have to offer. If you and a homeowner are standing on a great-looking lawn — sharply edged, growing and green — he or she will be open to your ideas for other ways to make the yard look even better. The customer is more than an item in your books, and more than a $200 per-month invoice. Your customer can be your partner in the effort to create something beautiful. Take time to look at each yard you service. Imagine what it can be. If you are continually educating yourself about landscaping, plants and other outdoor elements, ideas will pop into your head about this yard or that. Do not be shy about presenting your ideas to customers. Many of them will welcome your proposals, even though not all of them will have the money or inclination to accept your plans. But if you can up-sell one customer per month, you will do well.

Offering incentives is another good method to bring in more business from existing customers. People like value. When you offer to provide something for a reduced price, or even no cost, this can be a great way to convince a homeowner to give you more business. Call it "bundling services." If you are already cutting and edging the grass, spreading mulch in the spring, aerating the lawn, and providing chemical treatments, offer to weed the new flower garden for free or prune the bushes for a reduced price. After all, you are in their yard anyway, why not package more services into the weekly visit? While you want to avoid offering freebies to potential customers, who have not yet proved their value to you, your existing customers are a treasure worth treating well.

As your business grows, you will add to your list of services. You may offer only lawn maintenance during your first year in business, but the following spring you may be ready to prune bushes and trees or even plan and install flowerbeds, walkways, feeding and seeding, and other installation or maintenance essentials.

Always maintain a complete, written list of everything your company provides and regularly provide up-to-date copies to all of your customers. This list of services should be on your company's stationery or in the form of a professional-looking brochure, preferably with photographs of your work. In the beginning, you will not have anything to show, but as your business grows along with your customer base, you will have completed projects to display in your marketing materials. Be sure to get written permission from the homeowner before using any photographs of the property in advertising materials. This is known as an advertising photo release. A sample is available here: **www.asmp.org/ commerce/legal/releases/**

Whenever you add a service or product to your company's repertoire, tell your customers either in person, by mail, or by leaving a notice at their doors during your next visit. Add a personal note such as, "I am now providing bulbs and fall planting. I think your yard will look glorious in the spring when they bloom. Call me and I will give you a great price." Follow up later with a knock at the door or a brief phone call. Your customers have busy lives and concerns of their own, so do not assume they have no interest in the bulbs because they did not call. They may well be grateful that you took the time to remind them.

Up selling to new customers

For many people, coming face-to-face with someone who is trying to sell something is scary and unpleasant, even if they know or believe they need whatever product or service is on the table. Picture yourself ringing the doorbell. The customer answers and immediately makes a judgment about you, positive or negative. If you are a big guy, you should stand at a 45-degree angle in the doorway to avoid appearing to block the door. A 100-pound woman opening the door to 250-pound man will naturally be cautious. You do not want to be looming over her. You begin the trust process at that first moment of contact.

Smile, introduce yourself and ask what you can do for her or him. Listen to what is being said and consider how you can serve this person. Begin the up selling process at that moment. If the yard is a mess and the customer says all he or she wants is a one-time cleanup and mow, tell them you can do that and give them your one-time-only price, something higher than the price a similar customer would pay per week over the course of an entire season. Explain that you offer weekly or seasonal maintenance programs for every budget and offer to price out a seasonal or weekly plan for their yard. Point out specific areas that need work and offer to provide estimates to take care of these problems; for example, a weed-choked flower bed that can be cleaned up and mulched or a tree whose branches are dead or rubbing against the house and needs pruning. Be friendly, not preachy.

Try to provide the customer with a vision of what the yard can be. At that moment, he or she may only want the mess cleaned up, but perhaps what the customer wants (but does not believe is affordable) is a great-looking yard. You can provide that great lawn and garden, if only you get the chance. You have an opportunity to turn a skeptical, one-time-only homeowner into a loyal customer. You may have to build this trust one mow at a time, but you can to it. If the customer is willing to commit only to the cleanup, do a great job and chances are the customer will be open to more work from you. Even if you are working with a small-job customer, you still have the opportunity to do more.

This applies to first-time customers who are open to even more services at the beginning of your relationship — the type who is willing to sign up for a season of lawn care. This homeowner may not even have flowerbeds, a patio, or walkway to the back of the house, but over time you have the opportunity to provide them.

Flowerbeds offer more long-term profits than bushes because flowers need to be planted every year, bushes only once, and flowers need more maintenance. They must be purchased and planted every spring, then weeded, fed, and mulched. You can provide all of these services and more.

Selling products

Products offer great opportunities to up-sell your customers. The products you offer must be high quality and reasonably priced, at least as your target customer defines "reasonable". Someone living in a $3 million home will have a different definition of reasonable than someone living in a modest dwelling. You are probably looking for well-to-do homeowners who, ideally, are not shopping for flower bargains at the local big-box store.

One way to distinguish your company is quality. Your flowers may not be as cheap as the ones being offered by the flat in big-box stores, but they are of better quality.

Your business is seasonal, so you must plan it that way. In late winter, take a close look at your customers and what they purchase from you. Approach growers and suppliers for special pricing on whatever they offer, put packages together for your customers, and offer them as spring specials. You may find yourself with huge supplies of a certain kind of bush or flower that you are getting at deep discount — pass these along to your customers with whatever markup you need.

Ideally, you will have a relationship with your customers in which they become accustomed to your updates and offers without feeling pressured to buy everything you suggest. If they trust you and feel comfortable doing business with you, they will feel free to say no to what they do not want and reassured that what they do buy is good for them and their home. Over time, your business will flourish.

CASE STUDY: SKINNER NURSERIES, JENNIFER BROOKS

Skinner Nurseries
9150-4 Philips Highway
Jacksonville, Fl 32256
904-880-4344
www.skinnernurseries.com

Skinner Nurseries, the South's leading provider of green goods to the landscape construction industry, was founded in 1972. On twenty acres in Jacksonville, Bryant Skinner Sr. and his son Bryant Jr. began pioneering the concept of container grown trees in the South. After college, Russell Skinner, Bryant's younger brother and now president of the company, joined the firm as head of sales. Facing a tough economy in Florida at the time, they started selling container-grown live oaks in Las Vegas. During the 1980s, the market for container-grown trees exploded, and Skinner Nurseries grew along with it. Skinner's market was and remains wholesaling to landscape contractors, not the general public.

Over time much larger growing facilities and regionally placed distribution centers were introduced. Today Skinner services the entire Southeast, from Texas and Georgia to the Carolinas and of course, Florida — wherever live oaks grow. Spokesperson and Jacksonville market manager Jennifer Brooks says that, although the company downsized due to the economy, it still operates 13 distribution centers and 2 growing facilities. It also shrunk the somewhat bloated corporate structure. "We're back to selling trees and making money," she said.

Skinner's works closely with University of Florida and other advocates of horticultural education and plant science. Their service to landscape contractors features online ordering and lots of advice. For the nursery industry, it is very high-tech driven, with an automated purchasing system, total sales order system, and live inventory system. "We call it plant purchasing simplified. We offer everything from one-gallon grasses to 300-gallon trees to 10' caliper live oaks. All of our sales people, branch managers, and buyers are certified horticultural professionals in the states in which we work. We help customers pick trees, know the grades and standards for the municipalities that they work in," says Brooks.

Brooks loves the outdoors, and has spent her entire career in the industry, first with her stepfather's golf course installation, and now 14 years with Skinner's. "Oftentimes anybody who can afford a truck and a lawnmower thinks they're a landscape company," she said. "They're not. There's a lot of science that goes into trees and shrubs and watering and nutrients.

CASE STUDY: SKINNER NURSERIES, JENNIFER BROOKS

Those folks are exactly the people who are putting plants in the wrong areas, over fertilizing and over use of pesticides. You get a $1000 tree, you can't just dig a hole, stick it in the ground, and it will live. There's a science behind it. It can't be planted too deep. It has to have adequate water – 3 gallons of water per inch diameter, directly to the root ball. We do $100,000 and $200,000 projects with our contractors. They can't be losing $50,000 worth of materials. So I think the certification gives people confidence that when we tell you something we know what talking about."

Chapter Fourteen

To Focus or Expand

I t is your job as the business owner to know what is going on in every aspect of the company. That is, not only how the numbers look, but also who the customers are and what they contracted for. Which customers are ready to upgrade their contracts to more and pricier services? What is the status of bids and proposals? Which vendor has the best pricing this quarter? When was the oil in the truck changed? Do we have enough blades for the mowers? If you have employees, you will need to know what they were hired to do, what they need to be trained to do, and how many hours they work.

How will you know if it is time to expand your business or narrow it down to a tighter focus? For expansion, the rules are simple: if you are too busy to think, and you know you could get more customers or satisfy them better if you had more help, you need to expand. If you have had to turn jobs down because no one on your staff was able to perform them or had the proper expertise, but you do not want to add a subcontractor to the mix because that subcontractor is only partly under your "control," then you need to expand. For example, if you have been doing lawn maintenance exclusively for a while, and someone asks you to put in a flowerbed, it will be very tempting to expand into flowerbed installation. If you do not know the first thing about installing a flower bed, but take this customer's money but do a poor job at design, installation, and choice of plants. If the customer is unhappy, the word will get around. So if you decide to expand your services on a trial-and-error basis, at least do a thorough amount of research as you perform it. Maybe you will make less per hour on the project, but you will be broadening your skills and can reap the full reward you expect on subsequent projects.

Another factor that will tell you if you need to expand is if you are bored. Boredom can kill a business as fast as undercapitalizing it. If you feel weary and irritated all the time with your work, then consider what might cheer you up and breathe fresh life into your business. Whether it is learning masonry or adding wildflowers to your plant list, the expansion type is not nearly as important as how you feel about doing it. Everyone needs to feel excited and enthusiastic about his or her work, especially the person who is going the extra mile to run a business of his or her own. Life is too short. Do not let your work become drudgery. Open your mind, heart, and bank account to look at your business creatively again. You will find the right path.

Focusing or narrowing the scope of your business is the opposite of expansion. This may become necessary due to a tough economy, or feeling overwhelmed by too many different responsibilities. It may also be a matter of dollars and cents. If you evaluate the many different tasks you are doing, and notice that certain tasks are more profitable than others, you may choose to limit your business to the most profitable tasks that bring you the most satisfaction.

If you are reducing services, it is kind to your existing customers that you inform them of this fact in plenty of time, so that they can engage someone else. Also, you may want to draw up a list of outside sources they can contact. This may enhance your goodwill, not only with your customers but also with the firms to whom you refer.

For expansion or focusing advice, be sure to involve your accountant, banker, and possibly your attorney — as well as other advisors who seem to have a pragmatic attitude. Making impulsive decisions in any direction is usually a poor idea

Cutbacks in the economy often mean brutal times for existing businesses. Telling trusted employees they may be facing a layoff is never fun. Starting a business in a tough economy is more challenging than launching your venture when consumers are feeling prosperous in general, and banks are competing aggressively to loan you money.

There are some good reasons for starting a business during a recession though.

For one, you may have been laid off yourself, and are deciding to go off on your own because then no one can lay you off or fire you but yourself. If that is your situation, then what have you got to lose? It is certainly worth trying and testing yourself in the world of the self-employed.

Things are cheaper during recessions. There are more deals available when people are worried about money. You might even find an existing business that is for sale by a discouraged lawn care specialist, or used equipment that can save you a lot of money. Renting a garage to house your equipment may also be cheaper. You have to shop, of course — but when times are tough, there are opportunities for value. Auctions are everywhere. Not only could you purchase your truck at auction, quantities of equipment of every type is out there being unloaded by firms that are ready to call it quits. You may find some tremendous deals.

Being new, energetic, and enthusiastic, you may be better able to charm customers away from their former yard specialist. Giving your services away is never a good idea. You have to sell at market rates, but if you are operating from home your overhead is low. There may be some flexibility in pricing that will get you a full customer list even when the stock market is down.

Credit is still available, just harder to qualify for. You may be able to entice friends and relatives to invest in you — a known quantity — compared to a large corporate entity whose stock price has collapsed. You can offer your investors a reasonable rate of return. Ask your accountant to help you prepare a plan that you can show your personal friends and family that it will pay off for them in the future.

If you have a business going already, and it is suffering — the first thing you do is staunch the loss. Your accountant will have some thoughts about this. Scaling a business back for a while may be a viable way to keep it going in spite of the downturn. Merging with another company is a way to join forces to fight the rough economy together. The good news is, almost every recession through history has ended in less than a year, and the subsequent upturn averages 50 months of growth, before the cycle repeats itself. So by starting or forging ahead, even when the economy is bleak, you are pushing through the adversity instead of starting off in a deceptive cushion of easy cash. You will be fire-tested, stronger, wiser, and more determined to continue steering your business ahead. In the end, your business may do better because it was birthed in difficult times.

Appendix

Bibliography and Additional Resources

Statistics of US Businesses: 2006: US Landscaping Services

- **www.census.gov/epcd/susb/2006/us/US56173.HTM**

U.S. Small Business Administration Advocacy Small Business Statistics and Research

- **www.web.sba.gov/faqs/faqIndexAll.cfm?areaid=24**

2007 US Census of Agriculture- State Data –Table 35. Nursery, Floriculture, Sod, Mushrooms,Vegetable Seeds, and Propagative Materials Grown for Sale: 2007 and 2002 pps566-579

Five Characteristics of a Successful Business Owner

- **www.nfib.com**

Got What It Takes?

- **www.bizzia.com/startupspark/got-what-it-takes-find-out-with-this-quiz/**

How to Make Big Money Mowing Small Lawns, 4th Edition by Robert A. Welcome Authorhouse, Bloomington, IN ©2008

Start Your Own Lawncare Business by Entrepreneur Press and Eileen Figure Sandlin © 2003 by Entrepreneur Media Inc

Essential Plant Nutrients by Peter Motavalli, Thomas Marler, Frank Cruz and James McConnell College of Agriculture and Life Sciences University of Guam

- **www.cartage.org.lb/en/themes/Sciences/Botanical-Sciences/PlantHormones/EssentialPlant/EssentialPlant.htm**

Small Business Administration:

- **www.sba.gov/smallbusinessplanner/start/financestart-up/SERV_FINANBASICS.html**

- **www.sba.gov/smallbusinessplanner/start/financestart-up/SERV_HANDLE.html**

Immigration and Job Form Information

US Citizenship and Immigration Services

- www.uscis.gov/files/article/E1eng.pdf

- www.uscis.gov/files/article/E2eng.pdf

- www.uscis.gov/files/article/E3eng.pdf

- www.uscis.gov/files/article/E4eng.pdf

List of Forms Needed

- www.mbda.gov/?section_id=5&bucket_
  id=128&content_id=2335

H-2A Program

- www.uscis.gov/portal/site/uscis/menuitem.5af9bb95919
  f35e66f614176543f6d1a/?vgnextoid=28a634a57822e110V
  gnVCM1000004718190aRCRD&vgnextchannel=3381c0e
  d71f85110VgnVCM1000004718190aRCRD

- www.uscis.gov/portal/site/uscis/menuitem.5af9bb95919
  f35e66f614176543f6d1a/?vgnextoid=8f6434a57822e110Vg
  nVCM1000004718190aRCRD&vgnextchannel=3381c0ed
  71f85110VgnVCM1000004718190aRCRD

H-2B Program

- www.uscis.gov/portal/site/uscis/menuitem.5af9bb9591-
  9f35e66f614176543f6d1a/?vgnextoid=332cef590da4e110V
  gnVCM1000004718190aRCRD&vgnextchannel=91919c7
  755cb9010VgnVCM10000045f3d6a1RCRD

- www.uscis.gov/files/article/H-2B_18dec2008.pdf

Bonding

Specialized Insurance Company for Landscapers

- www.BearWiseLandscapers.com/

National Association of Surety Bond Producers

- www.nasbp.org/bond.cfm

Business community resources

- www.anla.org/

- www.lawnandlandscape.com/

- www.landcarenetwork.org/cms/home.html

Drug Testing

- http://business.uschamber.com/P05/P05_1075.asp

- www.laborandemploymentlawblog.com/2008/07/drug-testing-jo.html

Gardening

- www.gardenguides.com/

- www.weekendgardener.net/

- www.organic-gardening.net/

Government sites and forms

- http://business.gov/business-law/forms/

- www.epa.gov/oecaagct/

- www.irs.gov/formspubs/index.html

- www.nrcs.usda.gov/

- www.mda.state.md.us/

- www.maine.gov/agriculture/index.shtml

Landscaping

- http://tic.msu.edu/

- www.the-landscape-design-site.com/

- www.yardcare.com/

Marketing

- www.gopherforum.com

- www.wikihow.com/Write-a-Press-Release

- www.asmp.org/commerce/legal/releases/

Pest control

- www.common-garden-pests.com/

- www.ipm.ucdavis.edu/

- www.caes.uga.edu/extension/anr.html

Small business help

- www.asbdc-us.org/index.html

- www.johndeerelandscapes.com/_Professional_R_S/_Articles/Arti_mang_staff.asp

- www.sba.gov/

- www.toolkit.com/

Software

- www.accountingsoftwarereview.com/

- www.horticopia.com/

Supplies

- www.planetnatural.com/site/index.html

- www.miramarnurseries.com/index.shtml

Web site Design

- www.how-to-build-websites.com/

- www.webdevelopersnotes.com/

Index